CHANGING STEP

*From military to civilian life:
people in transition*

Also from Brassey's

JOLLY
Military Man, Family Man: Crown Property?

JESSUP
Breaking Ranks: Social Change in Military Communities

McINNES
Hot War, Cold War: The British Army's Way in
Warfare 1945–95

CENTRE FOR DEFENCE STUDIES
Brassey's Defence Yearbook 1996

LAFFIN
The World in Conflict: War Annual 7

CHANGING STEP

*From military to civilian life:
people in transition*

Ruth Jolly

Brassey's
London • Washington

First English Edition 1996

UK editorial offices: Brassey's Ltd, 33 John Street,
London WC1N 2AT
UK orders: Marston Book Services, PO Box 269,
Abingdon, OX14 4SD

North American orders: Brassey's Inc, PO Box 960,
Herndon, VA 22070, USA

Ruth Jolly has asserted her moral right to be
identified as the author of this work.

Library of Congress Cataloging in Publication Data
available

British Library Cataloguing in Publication Data
A catalogue record for this book is available from the
British Library

ISBN 1 85753 129 9 Hardcover

Typeset by M Rules
Printed in Great Britain by BPC Wheatons, Exeter

Contents

	Author's Note	vii
Chapter 1	*Changing Step*	1
Chapter 2	*The Military Experience: Expectations and Achievements*	18
Chapter 3	*The Military Experience: Institutionalisation*	35
Chapter 4	*Leaving: The Reason Why*	52
Chapter 5	*Leaving: Family Reactions*	69
Chapter 6	*New Occupations: In Quick or Slow Time?*	84
Chapter 7	*New Occupations: Traditional Routes or Unconventional Pathways?*	102
Chapter 8	*Wider Horizons: Goals Beyond Employment*	121
Chapter 9	*Family Complications*	135
Chapter 10	*The 'Gift of Continued Life': Conclusions*	151
Appendix	Basis for Structured Interview	167
	Further Reading	170
	Chapter Notes	172

Author's Note

Changing step: the process whereby an individual leaves the institutional framework of a military life and begins to build a new identity as a civilian.

The subject interested me for personal as well as academic reasons. Many years ago I trod this path myself. I served in the RAF for five enjoyable years but was ready and willing to leave when the time came. This, I thought, was too brief and too long ago to matter much any more. However, I gained some unexpected personal insights during the course of research, not least from contact with Jo Grant (who appears in the book) whose experiences partially parallel my own.

A more immediate personal interest stemmed from the fact that my husband was a member of the RAF and would inevitably leave it at some point. I therefore possessed ample motivation to investigate the puzzle as to why it is that some military leavers manage to adapt happily and completely to life as civilians while others never make the adjustment at all.

Case-study material was gathered by interview, and though most subjects were perfectly willing to be known by their real names, an important minority of interviewees whose experiences had been painful, understandably expressed a preference to remain anonymous. Names have consequently been changed in *every* case history, and personal details have been altered in a number of the more stressful stories. There are also some instances where a named individual is, in fact, a composite of two subjects, relating similar experiences. This device is useful since it confers an added degree of anonymity and facilitates direct quotation from a slightly wider range of interviewees than would otherwise have been possible.

A minor matter which nevertheless should be mentioned is the use of the pronoun 'he' to stand, on occasions, for 'he or she'. This phrase is too unwieldly to take constant repetition (in my opinion) and I trust the reader will accept the generic 'he' as a linguistic shorthand in these instances.

* * *

To the many people who helped me during the research and production of this book, I offer my sincere thanks. In particular, I am indebted to all those who agreed to be interviewed. Although not everyone who took part in the study has been directly quoted in the test, every single interview contained material which has informed its discussion.

I would also like to acknowledge the help I received from the Ministry of Defence public information service, and especially from Sqadron Leader Gerry Monte of that department. I am immensely grateful to Jenny Shaw and Caroline Bolton of Brassey's for their encouragement, their professional expertise and for their friendship. And, finally, I must thank my long-suffering and (mostly) uncomplaining family: Peter, Sarah, Tim and Charlie. I hope they – and you – find *Changing Step* as fascinating and worthwhile to read as it was to investigate and to write.

Ruth Jolly

CHAPTER 1

Changing Step

'Terrorists have murdered a young soldier in an explosion in County Armagh . . .', news flash, 15 May 1994.

Headline for a day, the tragic ending of a young life. Someone's son, someone's brother, someone's lover, he died, like many others, on peacekeeping duties. For a country not at war it is sobering to remember how many lives it costs to keep warfare at bay. Yet each person who chooses to make a career in the armed forces knows that this is the bottom line. In the course of their duties they may have to kill and they may die. Of course, no one thinks it will actually happen to *them*. They joined up for the camaraderie and adventure: to fly an aeroplane or drive a tank, to run their own show at an age when their civilian contemporaries were still sitting exams. Danger is part of the package. And if, at the checkpoint near the border – in Ireland, Bosnia or wherever they happen to be – they do not dwell on the possibility of ending their military service in a flag-draped coffin, they really cannot reflect too deeply on the prospect of ending their military service at all. That sort of thinking has to be saved for a quieter time. However, in today's leaner, streamlined, high-efficiency, fast turn-round forces, the quieter time may never come.

Michael C. left the Army in April 1994, a month before the young soldier died in Armagh. He knew all about the dangers of serving in Northern Ireland; he had been there too, and had taken charge of many a security operation close to the border with the Republic. Michael is in his thirties, married with three sons; a middle-ranking, middle-income, mid-career officer.

When the 1990 Defence Review *Options for Change* announced massive cuts in the armed services in response to the ending of the Cold War, Michael and his family knew there would be redundancies – but it wouldn't happen to them. The Army would ask for volunteers and plenty of other chaps would be happy to take the money and go. It might even work to their advantage . . . Michael was absorbed in a busy job at the Headquarters of the British Army of the Rhine when he heard that he was one of a number of candidates being actively considered for redundancy. Still, he couldn't really believe it would happen to him – until the letter arrived.

'He felt sick and angry and humiliated', said his wife. 'There were days when he frantically made decisions for our future which we had to reverse, and other days when he couldn't get himself into gear for anything.' The family flew home from Germany in a state of shock; assured of money, practical advice and some time to plan, but with their whole lives suddenly suspended in midstream.

★ ★ ★

Military service is a unique occupation. It is more than a job, not only a profession; it is a way of life. But a way of life that for most people ends well before they are contemplating retirement.

Changing Step looks at men (and some women) who chose to serve in the armed forces of the Crown but have now left, for a variety of reasons, and are pursuing other careers in civilian life. It asks why it is that some people seem eminently successful in making the transition while others remain for ever 'square pegs', uncomfortable as civilians, always 'ex-servicemen'.

Does it matter? Is it important whether or not a military man adjusts to civilian status? It is certain that some have no wish to do so – and what's wrong with being an ex-serviceman anyway? Only that it entraps an individual in his past and divests his subsequent endeavours of direction and intensity. At the extreme, a person can come to regard the rest of his or her life, with all its achievements, as an anti-climax. And that is a sad waste.

T.E. Lawrence (Lawrence of Arabia) wrote in 1926 with melancholy self-knowledge: 'Damascus had not seemed a sheath for my sword when I landed in Arabia: but its capture disclosed the exhaustion of my mainsprings of action . . .' He was not the first nor the last to leave the strong, clear world of the soldier to flounder in civilian life, never really to rebuild his lost sense of identity and purpose. Men of Lawrence's fame are few, but this aspect of his story must have a familiar and bitter ring to many former soldiers, sailors and airmen.

Adjustment then, does matter; it matters to future employers, colleagues and friends and, most of all, matters to the individual himself and his family. Unfortunately, adjustment isn't easy.

★ ★ ★

From initial training onwards, the armed forces mould their men and women, conditioning them to think and respond in ways appropriate to membership of a fighting team. Aspects of this training are not useful to individuals in other settings (if they were, there would be no need for such specialised training in the first place) and the required conditioning is intensive and often harsh. Rightly so. It is necessary for the military to devise this kind of treatment for willing subjects, for society is asking these people to be ready to fight and to kill and to die on its behalf – a tall order. The more so because although the military makes use of man's instinctively bellicose tendencies, modern warfare demands that these instincts be modified and, when necessary, overridden in order to fight successfully.

Instinctively, man is a social animal, and his co-operative behaviour is the very stuff of anthropological and sociological study. In a tribal context, the close personal bonding between members of a hunting and warrior band, their practised skills and corporate confidence enable them to face physical dangers unthinkable for an individual alone. Nevertheless, when they find themselves in mortal danger, a fight to the death is rare. Survival is paramount and should defeat loom, the instinct of the group is to flee.[1] Tribal groups, however, are more or less autonomous and clashes with other tribes are small in scale. Battles, on the other hand, are fought with collections of groups and it is often vital for one beleagured team to struggle on against impossible odds in order to give other, distant teams, time and advantage. This behaviour is *not* instinctive. It demands a cool-headed discipline which it is not possible to instil in the heat of conflict, but must be inculcated and reinforced in each individual from the moment of his entry into the military to the moment of exit.

But on exit, what then? What happens to the habit of subordination of self to the needs of the team when the individual leaves the Service to become a civilian once more? For though civilian life too is full of 'teams', the demands made by them are substantially different. Military leavers are offered much useful advice about employment, money and housing, but not a lot is said about 'deconditioning'. A leaver will eventually need to espouse rather different attitudes towards himself, his work, his colleagues and even his family – without at the same time rejecting all he has come to value, the ideals and standards which have become an essential part of his make-up.

To be successful in a second career and to achieve a reasonable measure of personal contentment a leaver '. . . must change not only to "fit in" but equally importantly, *not* to fit in . . .' (Frank Musgrove).[2] In other words, to have the confidence, when appropriate, to challenge the new system – and this requires not only competence in the job but also the 'insider's' sense of belonging which confers a right to criticise.

On every serving man and woman in the armed forces a great deal of time, effort and money is expended to make and sustain a military persona. When an individual leaves, however, he or she is faced with the inevitable erosion of this self-image. There is no one then to help the leaver to discard the military persona and to build upon its foundations a new social identity.

This, if accomplished to any degree, is a task accomplished alone.

* * *

Angus Moorcroft is a vet. A familiar figure in the Fenland town where he lives and works, it is hard to believe he was not born and raised there. Like many other veterinary practices, his business is geared to the treatment of domestic pets, but he has farm customers too. He is also an authority on the migration of birds, and his study, at the top of a tall, rambling town house, is crammed with ornithological data: books, charts and reams of computer print-out. His ambition is to be able one day to devote himself full-time to this work. Meanwhile, he and his wife Jane are much involved in local affairs. New acquaintances are often surprised to learn that the couple were Hampshire children, growing up near the sea, both from families with Royal Navy connections. And Angus's first serious career choice was military. Indeed, for 12 years as an RAF officer, the passion of his life was flying.

Frank Warrell left the Navy nine years ago, finding routes to career advancement blocked. He went to work for British Telecom. The years he has been with the company have been ones of corporate uncertainty and organisational change but Frank has prospered. A straightforward, down-to-earth sort of man, he exudes a quiet confidence and is clearly very much at ease in his well-paid management job. He and his family have made their home in the Midlands, far away from the seaports where he used to serve and they have lost touch with almost all of their former friends. Although he doesn't deliberately hide the fact, few people know or would guess that 20 years of Frank's life were spent in the Royal Navy, most of them at sea.

Jo Grant is a busy mother of twins. She is married to Chris, an Army Corporal. They met in Germany when she too was serving in the Army as a physical training instructor. After their marriage they worked for nearly two years at the same base, until Jo was posted back to England. Chris hoped to follow but trouble was brewing in the Middle East and eventually he was sent out to the Gulf. It was a watershed for the couple. Jo's initial contract of service was nearing completion and she had intended to apply to remain in the Army, with a view to combining a career with motherhood. In the event, the Gulf crisis placed Chris in danger and Jo found herself desperately regretting that they had postponed starting a family. Yet, as a soldier herself, she knew that if she had children, she could be separated from them in a military emergency. The anxious weeks of the Gulf War produced clarity out of turmoil for Jo, and by the time she was reunited with her husband she had decided to leave the Army. Today, she is an Army wife, bringing up children, living in married quarters, shopping in the NAAFI and helping at the HIVE. She is still with the Army, but no longer as an 'insider'. That part of her life is over and her role and status on camp are very different now.

Dave Lock is single, in his twenties. He was discharged from the Army four years ago, following a string of minor offences. A bit of a tearaway in adolescence, he had left home and was living with a friend's family when he joined up. At first, things went well and he thought he could look forward to a solid career. He joined an infantry regiment and found the training easy. But he developed a taste for alcohol – and alcohol is part and parcel of military culture. On nights out 'with the lads' he would invariably get into scrapes, and the scrapes became steadily more serious. Drunken brawls brought him convictions for criminal damage and assault, and in the end the Army decided he was a liability. He was out. Nowadays, drifting into and out of casual employment, losing lodgings when the rent is unpaid, sleeping rough in the summertime, alcohol remains Dave's preferred drug – but he'll use anything he can beg, steal or buy to blot out the despair. No one would imagine that this sad, shambling, unkempt youth was once a soldier.

Four very different people whom we shall meet again in the course of this book. Can we learn lessons from their experience? It would be useful to know how individuals who have adapted cheerfully to civilian life have actually gone about the task. Was it, in the main, a happy accident or did they consciously shape the process? Are particular talents necessary?

Or certain personality traits? And are some circumstances conducive to success while others produce more than their share of difficulties? The first step towards finding out was to go and talk to a wide cross-section of military leavers. . . .

* * *

A total of 62 people were interviewed in depth, at least 10 former officers and 10 former other-ranks from each of the three services. Apart from the fact that they had all freely chosen to make a career in the military (no National Service or Second World War interviewees) they were a very mixed bunch. Their ages ranged from 24 to 59, their length of service from 3 years to 36 years. They left under different circumstances from 3 to 24 years ago and they entered a wide variety of new occupations – from policeman to woodcarver, house-husband to entrepreneur.

They were asked a series of questions, designed to evoke memories, provoke discussion and test hypotheses (see Appendix 1). The hypotheses were derived from two sources: 'conventional wisdom', that is, oft-repeated but untested maxims and ideas which circulate in the military community, and serious academic research into the notion of social identity and ways in which it may change.

Thus where 'conventional wisdom' was concerned, a number of ideas were explored. It is thought, for example, that once change is embarked upon, the man who will succeed is the one who can put the past behind him and channel his energies as quickly and as single-mindedly as possible into a new venture. It is conventional wisdom that the young man with only a few years of military service under his belt will adjust to civilian life more easily than the veteran of 20 or more years' service; that the serious soldier who has seen much active service will find it harder to settle than the fellow who has only ever worked in a support role. It is believed that the man who takes a profession or a trade with him into civvy street has an advantage over the one who has to start again, and that a positive, optimistic attitude and an actively supportive family makes a vital contribution to the process of change. So say the 'common sense brigade'.

Moving to the area of previous research, there are some

good studies and interesting personal writings on the subject of a change of social identity under specific, though non-military, circumstances. For instance, there is information on individuals leaving a secular career to become ordained clergy[3] and, conversely, on people leaving a religious (monastic) life to rejoin the secular world.[4] There is material which focuses on homosexuals and trans-sexuals and the process of 'coming out'.[5] There is a study on men and women who left various walks of life to attempt to become full-time artists.[6] There is writing (much of it autobiographical) about the effects of emigration on personal identity[7] and there is also some interesting work concerning the adjustment of individuals in Third-World communities to the introduction of western-style work practices.[8] Equally interesting are investigations into the *preservation* of identity in adverse circumstances – as a prisoner[9] or a hostage[10] for example, or as a severely disabled person.[11] And all of this work is informed by well-known psychological research into the common human experiences of attachment, bereavement, loss and change.[12]

Reference will be made to some of these studies in later chapters, but suffice it to say that a number of findings recur in study after study and story after story. They show that, faced with the reality of a major life change, people have three options: they may make a conscious effort to alter their self-image in accordance with the new circumstances, or they may make a similarly conscious decision to resist any change to their image, ignoring the new circumstances. Or they may take a 'damage limitation' path. This involves a gradual acceptance of small differences while preserving continuity – at times an artificial continuity – with the past in as many ways as possible. It is clear that the active path of conscious change (or resistance) is hard, but it does produce results. People can and do change their sense of identity, notably when their sanity depends upon it or their convictions demand it. And they can change even in the teeth of unfavourable external circumstances or unhelpful personality traits.

However, given that this ability to change is present in all of us, it nevertheless has to be acknowledged that seldom does a life-change occur which is so radical as to *propel* an individual towards a conscious reshaping of his or her self-image. Most people's turning-points are more in the nature of long curves than right-angled bends, and most people can maintain the continuity of their lives without too much effort. As to changing themselves, it seems that people who can avoid thinking about it tend to evade the issue. Which is a shame, because the research also shows[13] that personal satisfaction is often impaired where life-change is handled half-heartedly so that a strong sense of identity is neither preserved nor rebuilt.

Looking at the interviewees' approach to their adapting to civilian life, questions were formulated with a strong emphasis on motivations: each subject's reasons for joining the military in the first place, his or her reasons for leaving, reasons for entering a chosen occupation, reasons for deciding to live in a particular place and in a certain way, and reasons for changes of mind.

* * *

Other people's research was also invaluable in highlighting three distinct stages in the process of change. For to move towards an altered perception of who one is in society, one's role, one's status, one's public behaviour and one's responsibilities is a complex business. Peter Marris, in his book *Loss and Change*, describes the individual's struggle to redefine the key meanings of his life in a new context:

> The ability to interpret events and predict from experience the outcome of behaviour is threatened. . . .he is caught between [the impulse] to return to the past, which seems in retrospect a haven of security and meaningful satisfactions; or to realise at once a new self. . . . Each impulse provokes its painful reaction: the attempt to revive the past only exposes its decay; the pursuit of the future leads to humiliating frustrations and bewilderment, and a sense of betrayal of his true identity. The conflict cannot be resolved, but only worked out . . .[14]

The first step in the process of change may be termed 'confrontation'. It consists of acknowledging and confronting the fact that an alteration of direction and lifestyle is desirable, or perhaps, inevitable. Two factors are important here: the degree of suddenness with which the realisation dawns and the degree of willingness to make a change.

Obviously, a person in shock needs time to recover some emotional equilibrium before he or she can move on to come to terms with the inevitability of change. Thus someone who is disabled through an accident has to confront the fact of the situation before any thoughts of adjustment can be entertained. The older person who, without warning, is made redundant or the youngster who fails to qualify for the profession he has set his heart on, has to deal with this cruel disappointment before any sensible action can be contemplated. Furthermore, such a morale-shattering event is a difficult starting-point from which to negotiate a major life-change. Nevertheless, in such circumstances, life *has* to change. The problem for many people is that confrontation can easily become selective. In some cases there may be long warning of impending change – the end of a contract of employment, for example – but no desire for it to happen and an inner denial that it will. In others there may be a strong wish to alter course but no immediate ability to initiate the change – for instance, when contractual or moral obligations to uphold the status quo are deemed, for the time being, paramount.

If confrontation is all too frequently partial and muddled, the second step, 'disengagement', is *always* muddled. Typically, disengagement starts in the mind, with a questioning of sympathies, of judgements, of priorities. As doubt and confusion over old loyalties and new directions mount, many people feel the need to withdraw from the source of the pressure and try to think in peace. This is where the long holiday, the retreat, the secondment or the sabbatical can play a crucial role. Having clarified attitudes and perhaps realigned sympathies, the individual may be ready to move in the desired direction – although movement at this stage is not always decisive and not always successful. Usually, as the person attempts to define what he or she really wants, mistakes are made and tentative fingers are burned. This whole period, when a former way of life is being relinquished before there are many certainties as to what will replace it, is almost always confusing and painful. But it appears to be a necessary and productive pain. The final break with the old way of life, when and if it comes, is often an anti-climax, a relief rather than a triumph.

The third step is 'Resocialisation'. Resocialisation is the business of assuming a new social identity – of becoming not so much someone else as something else – taking on a different role in society and, in doing so, being regarded differently by others and also by oneself.

It is somewhat comparable with being an actor, playing the squire or the butler, the soldier or the doctor, the convict or the priest. To give a convincing performance, the actor draws upon various aspects of his own personality and experience; often, this is so convincing that he has to subsequently guard against 'type-casting'. For the actor, a new role requires the depiction of a different kind of person in a superficial and limited fashion. An ordinary person, taking on a new role in life, begins in much the same way – going through the motions, acting *as though* he were competent in the new situation and adjusting his behaviour in response to other people's reactions. It is often said that the confidence of a doctor comes as much from being treated like one by patients as it does from the assurance gained from theoretical training.

Resocialisation is the final phase in 'changing step' – and it is every bit as difficult as the previous phases. It seems that people will not resocialise unless they really want to. Many change direction outwardly and vaguely hope that they will more or less fit in with their new environment and that others will make efforts to fit in with them. (Immigrants and pensioners may tend to fall into this mode of thinking, often with unhappy results.)

Even when change is desired, the speed of that change is dependant upon several factors. There is, for instance, the matter of the clarity of role models in the new role. Most people would have a fair idea of how they would expect a lawyer to look and behave, or a clergyman, or a plumber, but what about a poet? What about a step-parent? The clearer the notion of the 'typical' behaviour of the group one is intending to join, the easier it is to work towards it.

Then there is the matter of feedback. For a religious convert, communal worship helps him to practise his new faith with confidence. For those who change career direction, compulsory training not only confers skills but also helps a student to think and act like the professional he hopes to become. But where an individual is finding his own way without mentors, resocialisation will be hard – as Roger Middleton's study of would-be artists revealed.[15]

Finally, there is the depth and breadth of new training required to make the change – new qualifications, new concepts, new terminology, another language perhaps; for some, this can be a factor which extends the resocialisation period for a very long time – sometimes indefinitely.

Military leavers were therefore asked questions relating to the stages of change. What had triggered the realisation that their next step was to leave their Service? Were they able to begin to disengage soon afterwards? And what did disengagement involve? Did they think they had built, or begun to build a new identity? And, if so, did it just happen or was it a result of conscious effort?

As the process of adaptation progresses, outward adjustments, sometimes of an apparently superficial nature, start to proclaim inner change. A change in public name, with addition/subtraction/alteration of title is common. Changes in hair style and mode of dress are also common. Change may be manifested in the type and style of valued possessions: house, car, furniture and so forth. The way in which leisure time is used may also change under the influence of new friends and colleagues, as may such seemingly trivial matters as the kind of food and drink consumed and the social significance attached to meals. However, the most telling indicator of change is to be found in conversation. The enthusiasm with which the new way of life is described, the existence of new ambitions, and the extent to which detail and anecdote are employed to ensure that the listener comprehends, indicate a genuine commitment to the new path. This, plus an easy relationship with the past; to be able to talk in a calm and objective fashion about previous important events, without anger and without denial. These are good indicators of change, and if they all 'add up', there is little chance that the appearance of change is deceptive.

Military leavers were therefore given opportunities to describe their current styles of life as well as being invited to address past issues. For the validity of the conclusions drawn from interviews, this matter of indicators of change was vital. For, whilst we can all recognise change in people previously known to us, how are we to judge how much interviewees, never encountered before, had changed since leaving the military? And how can we estimate what degree of satisfaction their new way of life has brought them?

This is a similar problem to that faced by Michael Argyle when researching the subject of happiness, and a similar solution has been used.[16] Interviewees were asked – in different ways – how much they thought they had changed, what they had done to bring about this change and how satisfied they now felt with their lives. They were also questioned from the negative angle, about regret. As in Argyle's study, few people claimed complete contentment and even fewer admitted searingly painful regret. The majority took a mildly optimistic line, acknowledging mistakes and disappointments but painting a fairly comfortable picture of their current situation.

Given this 'average' baseline, each interviewee's estimation of the scale of his or her life change and the level of satisfaction it had brought, was compared with the 'indicators of change' which emerged from the interview. Where the two tallied pretty well, the subject's estimation was taken at face value – and these subjects were in a majority. Where there was a mismatch, it was taken to point to an element of self-deception in these matters. Not surprisingly, mismatching occurred most frequently over the satisfaction issue – where denial of disappointment seemed to be holding depression at bay: a necessary expedient. These are important defences and it would not have been helpful to have probed them. Thus there could occasionally be subjects whose self-assessment was erroneously taken at face value and others where mismatching led to a mistaken conclusion of self-deception.

* * *

The main work of interviewing took place between October 1993 and May 1994. Interviews lasted between one and two hours, depending upon the availability and the eagerness of the subject. As many of the questions were open-ended, there was scope for individuals to develop themes which were particularly relevant to their own stories – and some did so with great relish! When an interview drew to a close, it was quite common for the subject to express appreciation at having had an opportunity to recount his whole experience. A large number said they had never done so before and most seemed to find it enjoyable, even therapeutic.

And so to the initial outcome of the interviews; the broad results which would point the way to more detailed reflections.

The first result to emerge was that several of the hypotheses on which questions were based were clearly red herrings. That is, they were not so much untrue as irrelevant. What was thought to be cause was often effect. Much of the conventional wisdom was of this nature – superficially appealing but basically misleading.

One red herring was the hypothesis that the most 'adaptable' people are those who are able to put the past behind them quickly and to channel their energies into a new venture. This suggests that the past should purposely be ignored or forgotten – an idea which, even if it were possible, would be foolish. But it often *appears* to work. There are people who will claim that once they left the forces they 'never looked back'; and they are being truthful. However, in interview, their stories almost always reveal that the muddles and struggles of the confrontation and disengagement phases of life-change were endured while they were still in the military. Thus, on leaving, they were able to move quite rapidly into building a new future – the resocialisation phase. There were no short cuts, it was simply that leavers who had already begun the process of change had a head start over those who had it all still to do.

Another red herring was the issue of personality. The general idea that an extroverted optimist would manage change more easily than an introverted pessimist may be true but it is not particularly helpful. This is partly because in real life extremes of personality hardly exist – most of us lie in the middle ground *between* the opposites of introversion and extroversion, of optimism and pessimism. (Or of any other personality scale you care to mention.) Personality profiling would therefore have to be extraordinarily sophisticated to yield any consistent results. But more importantly, personality testing would still not provide useful information on coping strategies. And coping strategies are what we are looking for. So, while not denying the importance of personality to the individual, it is a line of enquiry unlikely to produce useful information for leavers in general.

But the biggest red herring of all turned out to be the whole question of whether it is easier or more difficult to adjust if the new occupation is allied to the military. One school of thought maintains that moving into an occupation such as the police, the prison service or the defence industries allows the new way of life to follow on, almost as a logical progression, causing little disruption and demanding no soul-searching. An opposing view argues that an allied occupation as a second career move will seem like a pale reflection of the military life which went before and will not give very much satisfaction. When you change step, it suggests, the step should be large, setting new challenges and opening new horizons. A seductive argument the latter, and one that seemed at first to be borne out by the interviews. Those who had moved farthest away from the military (the vet and the woodcarver, for example) were displaying many indicators of change and registering high levels of personal satisfaction. But wait; there was a small but significant number of people comfortably working in defence-related or uniformed public service jobs who had changed less, but whose levels of satisfaction were undeniably high. These people certainly did not feel that their current work was second-best; in fact, several said that they were happier there than they had been in the forces.

On closer investigation, the size of the step away from the military proved to be, of itself, beside the point. Of course, if a leaver chooses to do something radically different from his military career, the chances are that he has thought long and hard about it and is firmly committed to making it work. The lower risk option of an allied occupation is often (but not invariably) accompanied by a weaker commitment to the change. Thus it is not the nature of the new occupation which is crucial but the sincerity and power of the individual's attachment to it.

Moving from the hypotheses which did not stand up to those which did, it became clear that the nature of the individual's military experience *was* important, as was the manner of leaving it. Most (but not all) subjects who had adapted well, had had a generally satisfactory military career and had left more or less of their own accord.

The notion of three distinct stages of change, confrontation, disengagement and resocialisation, was borne out by interviewees' accounts of their progress, and the successful negotiation of each phase was seen to be vital. In particular, it was not possible to move directly from confrontation to resocialisation without going through some kind of a transition period. The use which could be made of this period was great, especially for those whose military experience had been unhappy. However, in practice, hardly anyone gave much thought to 'disengagement' or 'transition', let alone valued or planned it.

Finally, the desire to reach a new goal in civilian life was clearly crucial, and all the subjects who were well satisfied with their lot had formulated tangible, detailed and realistic aims for the future. They were looking ahead.

★ ★ ★

The following chapters take these findings as a way into the discussion as to how people leaving the military, successfully 'change step'. If, as it seems, it helps to have had a satisfactory military career, we ask what makes for 'satisfactory'? And what about distinctly *un*satisfactory elements in a military experience? Are some kinds of 'unfinished business' more difficult to deal with than others? We look at the new directions which people's lives have taken and the goals they have set themselves and ask whether some types of goal are more effective, more achievable than others. And if so, why?

In exploring these issues, we turn to individual stories, seeing how people actually lived through the process of 'changing step' – what they did, how they felt, what their families thought about it. People such as Angus, the vet, Frank, the manager, Jo, the young mother and Dave, the down-and-out, will enable us to make comparisons between the business of leaving the military and other, well-documented major life-changes. For, be assured, the transition from military to civilian status *is* a major life-change. It is, at times, frightening: 'More frightening than being on the streets of Northern Ireland', as one interviewee put it; but knowledge is a powerful antidote to fear. It is hoped that the accounts of how people have coped – for good or ill – will prove useful to others embarking upon the same journey. Most important of all, this book aims to discover and to pass on attitudes and actions which military leavers have found *helpful* in managing their own measures to 'change step'.

CHAPTER 2

The Military Experience: Expectations and Achievements

The phrase 'no regrets' is a cliché at the best of times but never more so than when uttered by former servicemen. No one leaves an occupation which has also been a way of life *without* regrets. Even the brightest of careers will have had its share of 'if onlys' and 'might-have-beens'. However, as indicated in the previous chapter, military leavers conform to the general premise that it is easier for people to depart without lasting regret when they have enjoyed a broadly satisfactory experience than it is for them to move on from an unpleasant or a disappointing time.

Despite the undoubted impetus which indignation can fuel, it is actually almost impossible to 'shake off the dust of your feet'[1] and not to dwell on failure at all. For human intelligence requires that we make sense of our ill-fortune. We need to know why things went wrong, how they happened and who was at fault. Only then can we explain to our own satisfaction the particular lack of achievement which hurts us; only then can we repair our damaged self-esteem and continue our lives in the confident assumption that we shall not repeat our mistakes. Clearly, the more serious the extent and depth of perceived failure, the harder it will be to explain, but until we have thought these things through, they will remain on our mental agenda as 'unfinished business'.

Some people, it is true, are able to relegate unfinished business to the back of their minds, but even there it demands attention from time to time. How many of us can still recall an insult or an injustice from schooldays with a burning intensity out of all proportion to the physical or psychological damage we actually sustained? If we are honest, most of us can. And we can still physically blush at the memory of our humiliation or seethe with anger at the unfairness of our unwarranted punishment.

Unfinished business, even of an apparently trivial nature, will periodically surface in the conscious mind seeking explanations, diverting concentration and sapping confidence with the re-emergence of unresolved feelings of helplessness. It is not surprising that those who have had a troubled military career are likely to be more encumbered with unresolved feelings of frustration and bitterness than those for whom the sun seemed always to shine. Moving on successfully may depend to a large degree upon the individual's ability to recognise and resolve unfinished business – but without doubt it helps a good deal to have only a small amount of such business *to* resolve.

When an individual has to confront the reality that his or her career in the military is going to end, the amount of disquiet this engenders does seem to depend upon that person's level of contentment with his or her achievements so far. Does this mean, therefore, that all retiring 'flag officers' (admirals, generals and air officers) feel smugly pleased with themselves while Bombardier Smith and Leading Seaman Jones labour under the burden of perceived failure? Clearly not, but if not purely a matter of rank and status attained, what is it that constitutes a 'satisfactory military career'?

★ ★ ★

'Achievement' means different things to different people, this much is certain. One man's successful career would be, in another's terms, a disappointment. However, the transcripts of leavers' responses show that a key measure of satisfaction is how well an individual's military experience has lived up to his or her original expectations of it – and these vary considerably from person to person.

No matter what 'acceptable' reasons applicants to the forces may cite for wishing to join (such as 'action', 'teamwork' or 'responsibility') people in fact have more complex and private perceptions of the rewards of a military way of life. And the interviewees who felt that, in retrospect, the military did give them what they were looking for on entry were the people who tended to rate their military experience most highly.

'What originally attracted you to military service?' seems a simple question but it often required a significant amount of delving to get beneath the pat replies. Many respondents had not thought deeply about the matter before, and some were faintly irritated to be pressed about it. However, where it was possible, it was useful to pursue their motives for joining up and to see whether their early hopes had been realised.

Angus Moorcroft, the vet, was one of a distinct group who *could* answer quickly and succinctly: 'I wanted to fly an aeroplane.' From boyhood he had been fascinated with aircraft but on leaving school he took his parents' advice and began a course in engineering. Quite soon, however, he realised that flying was more important to him, and that he could not settle for anything else – however sensible. Applications followed to the RAF and the Fleet Air Arm, and, when he finally entered the RAF, his delight in flying was enhanced, he says, for having had 'to work and wait for it'. For the next 12 years he was paid well and afforded much respect for doing a job which he loved. And although in the end he had to think about the future and whether the job would continue to absorb him for the whole of his working life, there was no doubt that for the period of his contract, the RAF lived up to expectations in full measure.

Angus was representative of a number of former aircrew and ex-sailors who had been attracted primarily by the natural element and the environment in which they wanted to work. They were excited by the sea and ships or the air and aeroplanes. 'I wanted to fly' or 'I wanted to go to sea' were common themes, and in both instances a military life had promised greater professional variety and a more adventurous lifestyle than civilians had. Interestingly, the attainment of this simple and straightforward ambition was reflected in the group's overwhelmingly contented reflections on their military experience, irrespective of other measures of career success.[2]

Frank Warrell, the British Telecom manager, had rather different motives for joining the Navy. He had no consuming interest in ships and had never lived near the sea. Nevertheless, the age-old temptation to run away to sea, to seek wider horizons and greater opportunities than home could offer, was what drew Frank into the forces.

The second-youngest in a large family, his future appeared to have been decided for him: 'Leave school, go into an apprenticeship, work in the factory, marry the girl-next-door et cetera, et cetera . . .' But he was an intelligent lad, he could have stayed on at school and entered higher education if that had ever been an option. The life mapped out for him was uninspiring and he felt he could do better, much better. But, lacking contacts, capital or family backing, where was he to turn? He joined the Navy, packing his belongings in a holdall and hitchhiking from the end of his street to the nearest railway station.

The military as a world of opportunity has always beckoned the able sons of the poor or disadvantaged. Caught young enough, the forces can mould the behaviour of their brightest recruits, use their skills and intelligence, and can instil in them a fierce sense of loyalty.

Like Frank, Michael C. (recently made redundant – see the previous chapter) joined the Army to find a freedom denied him at home. Michael's widowed mother had maintained that she could not afford to send him to university and had insisted that he should start in paid work. Underlying this, Michael realises, was her strong desire to keep him, her only child, at home. Michael responded with spirited defiance, applied for a cadetship and, at 18, found himself at Sandhurst. After that, the Army became his life, giving him career advancement, upward social mobility and an income sufficiently generous to enable him to make regular financial contributions to his mother. She, in turn, forgave his defection and was inordinately proud of his achievements. . . .

Many of the erstwhile clever youngsters looking for a better start in life found similar fortune. Frank, for instance, progressed more rapidly than he ever thought possible, though his new-found easiness of manner and his globe-trotting veneer of worldliness soon formed an almost impenetrable barrier between himself and his family at home. The military had given him 'a leg-up' as he'd wanted, but there was a price to pay. Furthermore, grateful though Frank and others like him remained to their Service, many hit disappointment later in their careers. For they did seem to find that, after the power-assisted start facilitated by their innate abilities and conscientious hard work, some years further on advancement slowed considerably and, for some, stopped altogether.

This is in the nature of things – the higher you go, the fewer the posts and the tougher the competition to land them. To climb the steeply hierarchical rank ladder it helps to have not only ability but also appropriate experience, background and, indeed, connections. Individuals who had joined in order to develop their potential were inclined to find that a new ceiling on their endeavours was galling, and a sense of frustration was inevitable. The reality is that, except in fireside tales, the cabin boy does not rise to become Admiral of the Fleet, however talented he may be. The military can give a capable recruit a flying start, but he or she has to know when to quit.

Jo Grant, 'Army wife' exemplifies members of another group, who joined the military with yet another set of expectations: 'I liked the life', she says. As, to all intents and purposes, she was raised in an Army family, she did know what that life entailed. Jo's mother was divorced when she was small, and from their earliest years, she and her brother spent a good deal of their time with their maternal grandparents on one Army camp or another. Grandfather was a senior NCO and Jo experienced a lot of the fun of a child's life on camp without the fearsome disruption of constant moves – it was her grandparents who did the moving. When her brother Matthew joined the Army, it seemed, she explains, a natural thing for her to follow suit. She felt comfortable in a military environment and wanted very much to belong, to be part of it.

The military attracts a large number of recruits from among the ranks of its own sons and daughters in much the same way as do other community occupations such as farming, fishing or mining. Military children grow up speaking the jargon, understanding the priorities and accustomed to the drawbacks of the life. A former RAF training-school flight commander says: 'They need less indoctrination . . . During initial training they're a help to the others . . . They teach them how to behave – what's expected in different sorts of circumstances. If they're suitably qualified and well-motivated they're ideal recruits.' Interviewees from this group had known pretty much what kind of life they were joining, they wanted it and, on the whole, they did not feel short-changed. Their expectations were realistic – and were realised. The problems which they encountered tended to occur later and to stem from their lack of close experience of any *alternative* way of life.

Before leaving the sons and daughters of military families it must also be noted that a proportion of them simply drift into the armed forces without having formulated a strong *personal* desire to do so. It is an obvious choice, acceptable to their families and safe. Furthermore, no one questions their motives and they are often too young, with too little life-experience to seriously question themselves.

John T., for example, had no idea what he wanted to do when he was at school. He was respectably academic, reasonably athletic, possessed a useful talent for drawing and painting and was outgoing and quite popular. His father was an admiral and his public school considered him the perfect kind of all-rounder to pursue a military career in his turn. While maintaining they had no desire to push him, his parents were nevertheless delighted with the idea that he should follow in his father's footsteps and John says that 'It all seemed so sensible. . . . Also, I didn't know what else to do, I didn't have another suggestion – pathetic really.' Dartmouth, too, considered him an excellent candidate and before he had finished school his progress through a gap year, university and on to

Dartmouth had been thoroughly organised. 'It was so easy, and I'm not saying it wasn't fun – but all along I knew I shouldn't have done it. . . . I thought about leaving all the time.'

So, why on earth did John enter the services when he clearly felt unhappy about it? An embarrassed pause, and John said slowly: 'I wanted to do something that would make people proud of me.' He did indeed make people proud, but it didn't do the trick. When pressed, John admitted that it wasn't simply his parents' admiration that he had craved, but their love – something he had never quite felt sure of. Facing the truth about his desperate need as a youngster 'to make people proud of me' was, by his own admission, a painful business. It involved recognising that he had felt rejected by his successful, preoccupied parents and unsupported by his two sisters, close to one another in age and interests. Doing well at public school hadn't been good enough; he had shone at the wrong things – art, for instance, and drama – and his father in particular had been unimpressed. So he had joined the Navy. But there is a world of difference between a course of action pursued for one's own satisfaction and one embarked upon chiefly to elicit approval from others. In the end, John horrified family and friends by suddenly (as it seemed to them) abandoning a highly successful career in early middle age.

Dave Lock, down-and-out, also joined the military to gain approval from others, though a different kind of approval. 'You get respect – as a soldier,' he maintained, 'you don't have people mess you about.'

Dave considers that he *was* 'messed about' as a child. His parents split up when he was four and his father disappeared from his life. Later, he lived with his grandparents, seldom seeing his mother; a lonely boy from his own account, watching hours of television and being frequently reprimanded 'for getting on me grandad's nerves.' When he was 10 he rejoined his mother who had married a man with two children, and Dave had to adjust to a whole new family. His own feelings and wishes, he believes, were 'never, ever' taken into consideration. In adolescence, however, he clearly found ways of making his presence felt. Loud-mouthed disobedience at school (when he was not playing truant), thieving from shops and offices, and a readiness to use his fists got him into minor trouble – and gained him a reputation for being 'hard'. He left home at 14 and went to live with a friend's family: 'They were into "The Brits" [the British National Party] and stuff. . . . A mate and me thought it would be a laugh to go and be mercenaries. . . . I joined the Army to get trained for it.'

In the event, Dave's Army experience did not launch him on the questionable career of the mercenary soldier, neither did it provide him with much respect, though it is difficult to know exactly what he meant by this word. At least he was not disregarded. Reading between the lines, it seems that his fellow squaddies in the regiment soon discovered that, given a 'skinful' Dave would do *anything* – the riskier the better – and, he claims, he never lacked for beer, dares or fights. He became known as 'a nutter' and 'a psycho' – dubious accolades but ones that he understood.

Unfortunately, what he *mis*understood was the Army. His vague aspiration to be a kind of street-kid with a gun was never going to be realised in the British Army. His need for constant attention and recognition was always going to run counter to the Army's requirements for teamwork and discipline. It is perhaps a matter for regret that this was not picked up sooner. Dave's reasons for becoming a soldier had everything to do with 'the image' (an inaccurate image as it turned out) and nothing to do with wanting the kind of life and work that the Army could actually offer. Small wonder that his experience fell far short of his expectations.

Dave's history is, of course, extreme. It would be wrong not to recognise that the armed forces have long been the salvation of many youngsters coming from troubled and deprived backgrounds. 'Stig', for instance, spent most of his childhood in care. He was not badly treated but lived in a total of five foster homes, never really settling anywhere. Without natural brothers or sisters and having only limited contact with his mother, he reckons that he joined the Army 'for comradeship' and adds 'to find a substitute family'. And he found it. He had a steady, unremarkable career which ended four years ago on completion of his engagement. The Army remains for Stig 'the best time of my life'. It gave him, he believes, stability, self-confidence, a sense of identity and a feeling of belonging which has stood him in good stead – but leaving was almost unbearably hard and he obviously still feels bereft.

The study revealed another slightly unorthodox but probably fairly common motive for joining the forces – that of meeting some form of personal challenge. A number of respondents, according to their own descriptions, seemed unlikely candidates for military careers but sought this path in order to 'prove themselves'. Paul is one of the most articulate:

'I was a shy, fat kid. You wouldn't believe it. A mother's boy but then so was my Dad . . . I was an only child . . . Not teased at school because I was cleverish – I think I was tolerated – left alone. . . . I didn't learn to ride a bike till I was in my teens . . . After that, I can't remember quite when, but I suddenly decided I *had* to do all these things. It was something to do with not wanting to grow up like my father. I went on an Outward Bound – camping, climbing . . . I was obsessional about it – I must have been an odd-ball . . . but I found to my amazement, I could do it.'

Paul was, to a degree, reinventing himself, and part and parcel of this was his resolution to join the Marines. His subsequent career in this branch of the services was as tough and as colourful as he could have wished. And despite the fact that, in time, he began to re-establish contact with that part of himself (the quiet, studious child) he had left behind, he remains sincerely grateful to the military for, as he sees it, 'normalising' him.

Paul's was by no means an isolated case, though he was unusually open and perceptive about the attraction which the military had exerted for him. Indeed, for a surprising number of respondents the challenge of acquiring a physical prowess and a level of confidence which they had previously assumed was beyond them was a factor in their decision to join up. Surprising, because it is usually taken for granted that only outgoing, naturally athletic, non-academic children will *want* to join the forces. Not so. The military clearly fascinates plenty of children such as Paul, who may seem at the time to possess little potential for teamwork, leadership or bravery. But if they wish it, somewhere along the line a combination of personal determination and sound training can produce outstandingly efficient, courageous and respected servicemen and women.

A different group of interviewees who were motivated by a desire to prove themselves was a small but highly significant one. Like the previous group, most of them tended to wrap up their primary motive in a host of more conventional explanations for wanting to join the forces. But these people's *main* interests and abilities were clearly intellectual. They were Thinkers. They had all performed extremely well in the education system and needed to use their well-honed brains. Outside the academic world, intellectual challenge can reliably be found in high-status, demanding professions such as medicine or law, or in the senior ranks of public service or private enterprise. Thus, when the Thinker joins the services, though interested in military matters, it is usually with the aim of getting to the top – and fast. (This, of course, is the author's statement; no one would or did admit to such single-minded ambition, so it *could* be a mistake to view certain interviewees in this light.)

In any case, the seven respondents who could be termed 'Thinkers', had a number of characteristics in common. They all left the military having achieved senior rank. They all professed great nostalgia for 'the sharp end' of the job (carried out by junior officers), but all had spent a minimum amount of time in such posts before proceeding to higher command. They all shared an obviously genuine enthusiasm for responsibility and an equally genuine interest in the more abstract areas of policy and planning. They were all *interesting* people.

The military needs some formidably intelligent individuals among its top brass, and young 'possibles' usually progress rapidly through the junior and middle ranks of their Service. But many never make it to the top. Disappointment is endemic in this group since almost all of them have at some stage to come to terms with less intelligent (although possibly more capable) colleagues being promoted over their heads. Feelings of frustration and failure are particularly marked in people who have opted for a full career in the military, been promoted to the 'No. 2' jobs but have been passed over for the top appointments. To ordinary mortals it may seem absurd that a major-general, a rear-admiral or an air vice-marshal could ever consider himself a failure, but no amount of previous success will ease the pain of rejection. And the fact that an intellectual inferior was preferred often provokes a reaction of unhappy bewilderment. Among the three interviewees of very senior status and four more of slightly lesser rank, there was a distinct feeling from them of having been *used*. As they were all extremely diplomatic in their comments, it is hard to put a finger on this. Perhaps it is that from schooldays onwards they had demonstrated their brainpower, taken pains to please – and got ahead – only to find that in the closing stages of the game, the rules had been changed and an outsider had won. They were left with the impression that the military had been only too pleased to use their talents – but that, after all, these weren't valued as highly as they had thought. It is inevitably conjecture.

The Thinker may leave the military feeling bruised and disappointed but it seems that the bruises do heal, and quite quickly. Despite advancing years they do not seem inclined to retire, and in a remarkably short time are able to turn their attention to new endeavours, be they in industry, private enterprise or academe. If this appears to contradict the notion that it is difficult to 'shake off the dust of your feet' perhaps it is the case that this small group *is* an exception.

* * *

The Thinker takes us from the idiosyncrasies of the nature of 'achievement' in individual terms to more conventional measures of success. The question as to whether the winning of prizes (in the form of awards and decorations) and the gaining of promotion does denote a 'satisfactory military career' needs asking. As expected, the answer is that, in general, it does. Most people who had demonstrably 'done well' were happy with their time in the military (provided the decision to leave had more or less been their own) and most of them seem to have carried their appetite for achievement into civilian life. As a group, albeit with exceptions, they can be seen to have prospered.[3] Moreover, many of these 'winners' evinced a characteristic attitude towards the military and related remarkably similar reactions to their experiences of military training, operations and their thoughts about leaving.

First, however, it should be emphasised that only a small number of 'winners' were primarily intellectuals. They were all quick-witted and were good, enthusiastic communicators; beyond this, their skills spanned the full range of practical, technical and administrative activities. They worked hard and were better at what they did than most of their contemporaries – hence the prizes and promotions.

They were an extraordinary and fascinating group, comprising a wide range of former ranks, of differing ages and backgrounds but expressing often startlingly similar attitudes towards service life. In particular, they were distinctive in maintaining a certain distance from their world, a degree of objectivity which was lacking in many of their fellows. It was not uncommon for them to have had difficulty fitting into military life. At the initial training stage many (even those from service families) appear to have been uncomfortable with the lack of privacy, resisted the pressure to conform and never quite accepted the military ethic whole. They nevertheless worked systematically and tended, quite rapidly, to do very well.

Some never planned to make the military their life's work (typically, the high-flying, short-service Army officer, aiming to move in his late twenties to a career in the City). Others adopted a wait-and-see attitude, enjoying success but remaining conscious of unfulfilled ambitions – not only in terms of promotion but also in terms of job and lifestyle satisfaction.[4] Many of those interviewed had decided to leave in their mid or late thirties – while there was still time to build a second career and to work towards the achievement of their remaining ambitions. They were usually the very people who, in the early stages, had won prizes, been put in key posts and had acquitted themselves well. Having experienced 'satisfactory military careers' to that point, many found it hard to explain to bemused family and friends why on earth they should want to quit.

Hugh P., for instance. An articulate, well-read young man, he entered the RAF slightly later than most of his contemporaries. Having joined a High Street bank after 'A' levels, he found that his life was 'boring and routine' and, despite assurances of a bright future in banking, he sought a more challenging career. Accepted for officer training at the age of 21, he felt very much older and more mature than his fellow cadets, most of whom were in their late teens.[5] As a result, he says, he held himself a little aloof from them. It helped him to cope with 'feeling out of it' without losing face and, while he missed some of the fun, he applied himself to the tasks in hand and ended by winning the top prize of the course, the sword of honour. As soon as he was posted to an RAF station, life became easier. In a more mixed environment with people of differing ages and experience he was able to relax and make real friends. His early feelings of isolation, he believes, made him sensitive to anxieties in others, and this helped him when managing a large number of subordinates. His facility with written and spoken English, his self-assured air of command (no longer aloofness) and his sharp-eared and sharp-eyed concern with the problems and difficulties of those working for him made him an excellent boss. His teams performed well and he deservedly reaped the rewards of rapid promotion to the rank of squadron leader.

At that point, however, he began to weigh up his situation. He was not aircrew and was therefore not very likely to reach the highest ranks of the force; he was bright and ambitious but there were no short cuts; in particular, there was no way he could avoid the duller jobs in his branch if he wanted to 'get on'. Moreover, he was, by now, married with school-aged children, and the idea of settling down in one place was attractive to the whole family. So, to the amazement of colleagues, Hugh decided to leave. He now works at the headquarters of an international aid agency. It is an exciting, demanding job, 'morally right' and he loves it – though it pays less than the RAF. His experience in logistics and familiarity with the pressures of emergency situations have been invaluable to him and he regards his time with the RAF as having been both enjoyable in itself and a vital preparation for the work which he does now. A satisfactory military career, in his view, taken a step further; but, with a rueful smile, he admits that some former associates would say that it was a satisfactory career wasted.

Unlike Hugh, Dr Alison M. never intended to wait and see how her career developed. As a medical student she participated in Operation Raleigh (now Raleigh International) and worked in tropical jungle alongside an Army doctor. The experience was, she says 'mind-blowing' and as it came to an end she decided to try and extend herself in a similar way after qualifying and before settling down. She signed on for a minimum engagement, accepted every professional challenge that came her way and was soon offered the chance to change her terms of service to a full career. She refused. 'I was flattered but I always planned to go back into [medical] research.'

The military for Alison was an invigorating diversion. She used it and was used *by* it but was never tempted to stay. Although enthusiastic about the range of opportunities available to junior medics, she could, in her opinion, see these diminishing rapidly for more senior practitioners – and for women in particular. Today, she looks back on her time in the military with great affection but has no doubts about the wisdom of keeping her contract short.

The study suggests a paradox that prizewinners and promotees are often *not* the most securely integrated members of the forces. Many of them expressed feelings of being 'on the fringe' of their peer-group, despite having enjoyed their years of military service. It is perhaps not surprising that most seem to have made the transition to civilian life with typical thoroughness. They generally found that they still possessed the determination that took them so far so fast in their military careers. Those whose ambitions had subsequently been thwarted had frequently discovered an even keener desire to succeed, and their industrious, enthusiastic wholeheartedness had become the key to their adaptation to new and different working cultures.

★ ★ ★

So, what has been discovered? That clever people with clear ambitions who have worked hard, won prizes and got ahead have had 'satisfactory military careers'? This is not surprising. That their ability to motivate themselves and their obvious need for tangible achievements can carry them through the difficult transition from a military to a civilian mode of life? That they adapt because they have a drive for success which *compels* them to? Such people include Frank Powell, Hugh P. the aid worker, and Dr Alison M. It is an interesting finding – but not, one has to admit, immediately useful. For prizewinners, promotees, 'high-flyers', 'fast-runners', 'winners', call them what you will, make up only a small minority of any organisation, and the armed forces are no exception. Nevertheless, we may learn from this group. We shall discover that, as individuals, their progress through the phases of 'confrontation', 'disengagement' and 'resocialisation' was no less painful than other people's, but they were *driven*. Most of them did complete a kind of metamorphosis, coming across not as ex-servicemen and women but very much as their present and future selves. A metamorphosis that many others would like to emulate.

We have also defined a wider group who enjoyed satisfactory military careers. These were the individuals who had found whatever they were looking for when they chose to join the forces. Thus to the obvious 'winners' we may add people such as Angus Moorcroft, who simply wanted to fly, Jo Grant, who wanted to belong to and live in a military world, Stig, who, in the communal life of the Army, sought a substitute family, and Paul, the product of an overprotected childhood, who longed for adventure and physical challenge.

Because many respondents found it difficult to describe the often mixed motives which brought them into the services, it was sometimes impossible to determine the primary reason for their choice. This in turn made it impossible to tell whether their aspirations had or had not been realised. Interviewees, when stumped for an answer, turned readily to the stock explanations they had always used when asked why they wanted or *had* wanted to join up. It did not seem that these reasons had been much questioned by others, and individuals varied enormously in their degree of perspicacity and self-knowledge on the subject.

It is, however, an exercise which people can perform for themselves. To ask: 'What attracted me to military service in the first place?' is likely initially to generate a cluster of interrelated answers. But given time and persistence ('What was it I *really hoped* I'd find?') the answer should become simpler and clearer. Then the follow-up question: 'Did I find it?' . . . 'Absolutely?' . . . 'Partially?' or 'Not at all?'

The subjects in the study who could to some extent describe what they had wanted yet failed to find it in the military were small in number but instructive. People such as John T. and Dave Lock. Two men as different from one another as chalk from cheese – and yet sharing similarly crossed wires; both wanting something from the military that was essentially irrational. John's primary reason for going to Dartmouth was to attempt to gain his parents' love and approval. Regardless of what he had told the Navy Selection Board, that was his *real* motive for putting on a dark blue uniform, and it was, he came to see, 'crazy'. Public life, a career, is the wrong medium through which to pursue a quest for parental love. It could not have succeeded and it did not.

Dave, too, was chasing a fantasy. He sought attention, 'respect' – and lots of it – all the notice and affection he had missed as a child and had achieved only fleetingly later. But again, a career is not the best sphere in which to strive after an emotional goal. Neither man enjoyed his time in the military as a whole, although they both took pleasure in some aspects of it. When asked to recall their confrontation with the fact that they would not complete their service, each recounted feelings of bitterness and a sense of time wasted.

One important strand of a satisfactory military career is, therefore, that it should have lived up to one's initial expectations (whatever they may have been) and that, if possible, it should have produced recognition in the form of prizes and/or promotion along the way. For the lucky, the sensible, the realistic ones, this kind of experience did help the process of letting go when the time was right. Wanting more from life is not the same as feeling short-changed or hard-done-by, and those who had at least achieved their original goals were able, by and large, to confront the prospect of leaving with equanimity.

CHAPTER 3

The Military Experience: Institutionalisation

In the words of a former Principal Psychologist to the Navy: 'To understand the end you must go back to the beginning. . . . In those first six to eight weeks in the forces, new entrants are put through a programme of incredible intensity which affects them for life.'[1]

The practice of taking a willing but callow youth and initiating him into a hunter/warrior caste is basic to most societies. Though adjusted and refined for twentieth century needs, the techniques employed cross barriers of culture and time and continue to produce a profound effect on those who undergo initiation. The process has evolved as a masculine rite of passage – since warrior-bands have been almost exclusively male – and it is hard to know whether modern women sharing the same experience actually *feel* the same about it as their male companions. They certainly react in similar ways.

Initiation, of course, is just a beginning: the first step towards a new way of *being*. But as in other fields (notably the religious life), the first step is the largest, the initial commitment the most telling.

In anthropological terms, what happens is this. The initiate is removed from his home and family and is placed in the company of other initiates and mentors. During the period which follows he completely submits himself, day and night, to a programme of instruction which demonstrates his inadequacies, teaches him the customs and practices of the group, puts him to the test and either accepts or rejects him. At the end, the accepted ones emerge in ceremonial rebirth, as warriors.

In ordinary parlance, young men and women accepted for basic training in the military leave their homes, families and friends and go to live on a training base – an enclosed community where contact with the outside world is limited. There, for a while, they surrender control over virtually every aspect of their lives to those in authority over them. They are shown their inadequacies, they are taught the customs and practices of their Service, they are put to the test.

The system sets out first of all to humble the recruit. Symbols of individuality are ignored or prohibited. No unusual clothes or unorthodox hairstyle, no jewellery, no going out without permission, no first name. Instead, a uniform, a rank, a surname and a number; drill, bull and inspections. So how does it feel to be constantly scrutinised – dress, bearing, kit, bed-space – and found wanting? To be shouted at, reviled, to be punished for transgressions of rules only half-understood and to take it calmly, behaving all the time with careful deference to the tormentors? It is humbling; even, at times, humiliating; and no recruit escapes some loss of self-esteem. Now add to feelings of inadequacy, a fear of failure. For those who are not going to measure up, rejection comes swiftly and privately. Taken aside, they are interviewed, given reasons, condolences and good wishes for the future – and then they are gone. For them, it is over quickly, but it has an alarming impact on those left behind.

Self-confidence shaken, painfully aware of their shortcomings, the recruits are taught. The body of wisdom imparted to any group of initiates is invariably a rich mixture of good sense, good practice, specialist knowledge, myths, symbols, rituals – and not a little superstition and mumbo-jumbo. Its acquisition is generally made easier if it is swallowed whole, with a minimal application of critical judgement. As teaching is received and acted upon, certain behaviours start to become habitual and a range of attitudes is taken for granted. The trainees begin to bind together as a group.

Cementing the group bond and transforming the link between the group and its teachers is the purpose of the third element of the initiation process, that of being put to the test: ordeal. Ordeal has a long pedigree in these matters. The obligatory and terrifying climbing of the mast at the old naval training establishment of HMS *Ganges* (still vividly recalled by many a former sailor) stands in direct line of descent from ancient tribal initiation practices. The difference between ancient and modern custom is that modern military ordeals do insist upon there being some resemblance to situations which may, *in extremis*, be encountered operationally. Thus a valid 'training' label may be affixed to those exercises which demand physical courage, teamwork and a determined imperviousness to fatigue and pain.

It is thus in the name of training that recruits are required to scramble up slippery rock-faces with packs on their backs, to jump across chasms, swim through submerged pipes and so on, each member of the team attempting to repress his or her own fear for the benefit of the others. Inevitably, nerves fail, injuries occur, exhaustion sets in; but the teams bind together, each member now willing and helping the rest to succeed. And the instructors miraculously turn from hectoring tyrants into desperate coaches, yelling for joy when a task is completed, urging the team on when a target is missed.

If the exercises go well, the trainees, living on their wits, putting their trust in their companions and working together, will discover that they can overcome fear to carry out tasks impossible for a lone operator. The subordination of the individual to the group begins to be accomplished.

And so to the passing-out parade: rebirth. A solemn ceremony to which friends and family are invited and at which they bear witness to the transformation which has occurred. As yet, of course, the change is not all-pervasive – and for some people it never will be – but neither is it superficial. A threshold has been crossed and what has been done, cannot be undone.

Many tribal societies require their warriors to undergo ritual ordeals at intervals throughout their active lives. In the same way, military men and women are, from time to time, obliged to set aside their normal duties in order to receive further instruction and testing. (Not the kind of in-service training recognisable to most civilians, though that, too, exists.) Command courses, survival courses, ceremonial commitments, expedition training and exercises – planned or sprung without warning – all of these continue to perform the dual function of maintaining emergency readiness and keeping strong the bonding between servicemen.

To have entered the military from choice, to have been selected, initiated and to have had that initiation repeatedly reinforced, is to have become a military man or woman. To have then carried out operational tasks, to have served in dangerous places and, possibly, to have fought, is to have lived the military life. Having committed so much, having achieved full working membership of the organisation, having trusted it and, in return, having been deemed trustworthy, it is a serious matter indeed to contemplate leaving it. For the military incorporates the *identities* of its members, and when they leave, they have somehow to rediscover themselves as separate, self-motivating, vulnerable individuals.

★ ★ ★

Phil is typical of the homeless ex-servicemen described in a new study, 'Falling Out', commissioned by the homeless charity Crisis, which reveals that up to a quarter of people on the streets have done military service . . . Brought up in an Army family – his father is an officer – he now believes serving his country was a waste of time and that the 'institutionalisation' rendered him useless in the real world. 'In the Army there are people to sort out all your problems. But as soon as they get you out the door they just don't want to know.'

(*Independent on Sunday*, 29 May 1984)

There is a strong public perception that the military institutionalises its personnel, making adaptation to civilian life when they leave very difficult. This perception is not fallacious but, like many half-truths, it demands more careful analysis.

Nobody would dispute that an institutionalised person would indeed find life outside his institution hard, if not impossible. Being institutionalised, strictly speaking, involves a total yielding of the self to an organisation, to the extent that the self hardly exists as a separate entity. And the hallmark of such a person is his complete lack of self-motivation, which results in apathy when the routines of institutional life are withdrawn.[2]

Fully institutionalised people may be found among the ranks of long-term prisoners, residents of homes for the physically or mentally handicapped, in homes for the elderly, and nursing home and long-stay hospital patients. All of these people have, for one reason or another, *lost* the freedom to order their own lives and have become incapable of looking after themselves. Military personnel are not institutionalised in this way. However, like members of monastic orders, they have *surrendered* a large proportion of control over their lives and have pledged obedience to their superiors. Since they have submitted of their own volition, their self-esteem remains intact and their perception of dependency is not great. Unlike the prisoners, the sick and the disabled, they usually feel enriched, not defeated, by the organisation which directs their endeavours. They remain motivated, from choice, to live their lives according to rules to which they have given their assent. And when they leave, they leave not as 'losers' but as former members of a body which commands widespread public respect.

But if the element of free will guards military men and women against total institutionalisation, the existence of a large corpus of rules and regulations, of standardised surroundings and equipment, of the need to subscribe to a group mentality, of the security of hierarchy within which both the habit of command and the acceptance of orders is unquestioned, does undoubtedly predispose them towards a significant degree of institutionalisation. It is not so much that military leavers are *unable* to do the many things which may be done for them in the forces (such as organising their accommodation, applying for work, and negotiating pay and conditions) but that they can find it hard to initiate activities in an environment which seems alien, even hostile. Ray McKnight, manager of a London Day Centre which helps many ex-servicemen, puts it succinctly when he says: 'They don't feel they belong anywhere. They are *psychologically* homeless.'

If it is any comfort, this is an experience fully shared by individuals who leave monastic communities. Karen Armstrong, for example, a highly educated, well-organised woman, found it extraordinarily difficult to cope with even the simplest and most humdrum of tasks in the unfamiliar world outside her convent:

> I was now 'free' to fall in love, to travel, to enjoy all manner of sensuous and spiritual delights that had hitherto seemed closed to me. Yet the convent was where every bit of me belonged . . . I still tried to lift the heavy skirt of my habit when I went up a flight of stairs. My hands constantly fumbled for the long ceremonial sleeves to hide in . . .
>
> I thought back to the meals I'd cooked in the convent, the water-logged vegetables, the custard made with powdered milk. As I stared, glassy-eyed at elaborate magazine photographs of crown roast and charlotte russe, my heart sank . . .
>
> I felt a sick panic, continually throbbing just below the surface. I was afraid I wouldn't be able to cope with the demands of this strange new world, that I'd never be able to adapt.[3]

Again, Anthony Kenny, who left the priesthood for academe and marriage admits:

'It took a while to overcome an initial agoraphobia after laicization. I dreaded the first encounters with friends . . .'[4]

It is not inability which inhibits coping but a self-protecting impulse to lie low while attempting to get the measure of a new situation. Unfortunately, in modern society a person who drops out of the fast pace of everyday existence may find it difficult, even impossible, to re-enter.

Among the military leavers interviewed there was no shortage of evidence of institutionalisation, from a mild to quite a marked extent. At one end of the spectrum were individuals who were simply not coping; people such as Phil Battersby, the former Guardsman featured in the *Independent on Sunday* and Dave

Lock, living rough and spending whatever money he could find on drugs or alcohol. At the other end were a far larger number of leavers whose institutionalisation was indubitable but moderate in its depth and effects. The continuing emotional dependence on the military of these respondents was manifested in their keenness to talk about the past, contrasting sharply with their prosaic descriptions of the present (including interviewees for whom present circumstances were actually very favourable) and an attitude of indifference or even pessimism towards the future.

During the course of each interview, subjects were asked to describe two or three of their most vivid memories of service life. Once they had begun, a great many people found it impossible to restrict themselves to just two or three memories and did, in fact, talk at length about their military experiences. (This was such a problem at first that the order of the interview format was changed so that this question was put near the end of the discussion – a few of the early interviews having been severely hampered by a lack of time to properly explore the subject's current lifestyle and hopes for the future.)

Of those who were almost unstoppable in their tales of service life, a smallish but nevertheless disturbing number were also unenthusiastic about their lives since then. They displayed a sense of purposelessness, of inadequacy, of the good times having gone, of resignation to their present lot and an absence of goals for the future. This group shaded into a more representative body of people who, although equally ready to regale a willing listener with reminiscences, were able to view their new lives with some optimism and to formulate some aims, the achievement of which would give them pleasure.[5] But many of this group too, were of the opinion that the military years were the *best* years, that they would never again have quite so much fun, so much excitement nor so genuine an experience of comradeship, and that these things – fun, excitement and comradeship – do indeed constitute the best of life. There was a certain stoical sadness in a lot of people, bound up with feelings of lost youth and vanished ideals.

* * *

Given that the military does institutionalise its members, the question then arises as to why not all servicemen and women are institutionalised to the same degree. For, while a fair proportion of interviewees were still, some years after leaving the forces, showing signs of emotional dependence on their Service, by the same token, a good number were not. How was it then that while some people seemed to have carried their military conditioning over into civilian life, others had clearly distanced themselves from it? Who were the 'deconditioned' ones and how had they moved away from the military 'mind-set'? How had they ceased to relish the life of communal endeavour within strict but secure boundaries when many of their former associates continued to cleave to this ideal?

The obvious hypothesis was that members of the armed forces would have become progressively more attached to the military way of life the longer they were exposed to it. If so, there should be a correlation between long service and institutionalisation.

Another thought was that their attachment would have been strengthened by the experience of active service – operations 'for real' as opposed to training exercises. That people who had repeatedly put their training into practice (in peacekeeping situations, in delivering humanitarian aid, in providing fishery protection or search and rescue, and, for some, in combat) would be more conventionally military in outlook than those who had seen little action. If so, there should be a correlation between active service and institutionalisation .

There was no correlation. No correlation between either long service or active service and institutionalisation. In fact, the more extreme kinds of active service seemed, if anything, to have had the reverse effect.

Take Alan C. If anyone was going to be institutionalised, it should surely have been he – a 59 year old retired Group Captain who had been in the RAF for his entire working life to the age of 54. He entered Cranwell straight from school and was involved in operations at all stages of his career – as a young aircraft captain, as a squadron commander and as a station commander. And yet, only five years after leaving the RAF he estimates that few of his new friends and neighbours are aware of his service background. His second career – in tourism – is a small scale venture, pursued with the confidence of one who possesses some financial security (an advantage he has over younger, more junior leavers), but the infectious enthusiasm with which he describes his new horizons is astonishing.

On the other hand, there is Stig – mentioned before. A soldier for 10 years, still a young man with everything to strive for. A successful stint in the Army, moderate promotion (he became a junior NCO), some time spent in a support role in the Falklands but nothing too dangerous, nothing traumatic in the way of action. A short, satisfactory career, and one which he greatly enjoyed – especially the experience of comradeship. He learned a lot both socially and professionally and came out at the end of his contract with money in his pocket. Just the sort of fellow who should surely be able to take his service experience and build on it as a civilian. But four years later, he is still struggling. On his third job since leaving the Army, he is no nearer to finding an occupation which he enjoys. Living back in his old home-town, he feels something of a misfit but is nonetheless reluctant to move away from the security it provides. He is not without hope, certainly not clinically depressed, but says he is 'drifting' – still looking for a way of life to embrace wholeheartedly, still missing the Army.

Alan C. and Stig are but two examples of people who give the lie to the notion that becoming emotionally dependent on the forces is either simply a matter of time, or else a matter of being frequently operationally involved in its activities. We know that the military tends to intitutionalise, so it is perhaps more of a puzzle that Alan C. has deconditioned himself than that Stig has not. It would be useful to know what factors were operating for Alan that were not working for Stig.

★ ★ ★

One clue to Stig's continuing attachment to the Army comes from other research in the field of institutions and their effects on individuals. A well-known study which demonstrates people's capacity to remain impervious to altered circumstances and *not* allow themselves to adapt, is Cohen and Taylor's study of E wing at Durham Gaol.[6] The two researchers visited the prison weekly for a period of approximately four years and spent time with 30 or so medium-term prisoners there. The work which resulted was entitled *Psychological Survival* and related how inmates were able to maintain their overriding desire 'to be the same person on leaving prison as on arrival'. Despite real degradation and punishment, lack of privacy and shortage of useful occupation, this ambition in itself gave a sense of purpose. Physical fitness training, adult education classes – anything which could absorb blocks of time and provide evidence of progress they used to bolster their self-esteem and to nourish the fantasy that the prisoners were an elite, guarded by mindless officers, beneath contempt. The extent of institutionalisation among these prisoners was far less than Cohen and Taylor had expected:

'We have asserted that the men in E wing hardly lost their identities as a result of being processed through the prison system.' This, despite 'a massive and prolonged assault on their sense of identity'.

These findings are supported by less formal prison research such as James Campbell's *Gate Fever*[7] which looked at life in Lewes Prison. Again, case studies indicated a marked retention of personal identity and included several interesting descriptions of the ways in which inmates decorated their cells with posters, pictures and newspaper cuttings, loudly proclaiming their own tastes and almost always photographs of themselves *as they were*.

This work presents some striking similarities with a study conducted by Frank Musgrove in another kind of institution – a Cheshire Home for the severely physically disabled.[8] All but two of the residents had been healthy working adults earlier in their lives. Now a majority were suffering degenerative conditions of the nervous system while a smaller number had been paralysed as a result of accidents. All were dependant on wheelchairs for mobility and had little control over their limbs.

Unlike the prisoners, the Cheshire Home residents had willingly entered the institution and most regarded it not just as a sanctuary but as a real home. Tragically, their lives had altered beyond all recognition from former patterns. Many felt that their personalities had had to become quieter, more patient, more tolerant both of themselves and of others. But their sense of identity remained resolutely unchanged – even across some 30 years or more of disablement.

Residents continued to define themselves in terms of occupation. When asked how life had changed since their accident or illness, residents would invariably ignore their years of incapacity and talk immediately about their 'normal' past. A schoolmistress:

'Well, the big change really was nearly 12 years ago, when I had to give up my job as a teacher.' And she continued to chat with animation about school life – as did a former ship's cook about sea-time, a slaughterman 15 years away from his work and indeed a master mechanic who had to terminate his employment 30 years before.

'From the receding margin of the world, modest occupations relinquished decades ago provide a reference for the whole of life and seem to grow rather than diminish in significance.'

In similar vein, sexual activity was out of the question for most residents, but, although the staff recognised this and treated them as 'essentially sexless' people, they took no account of this treatment themselves. There was still flirting between men and women; the women in particular went to a lot of trouble to look not just presentable but attractive, and the men still boasted of sexual conquests.

Like the prisoners, these residents drew strength from regarding themselves as an elite – braver and stronger-willed but more tolerant and with greater insight than most people. Like the prisoners, their psychological survival depended upon their remaining 'normal' and rejecting all the inevitable pressures from the rest of the world to marginalise them.

* * *

The insights provided by these pieces of research begin to throw some light on the paradoxical situations of some military leavers. They indicate that, when people find themselves in an environment where they feel out of place, they continue to use the memory of their previous environment as a frame of reference. Normally, this will be only as a temporary measure while they adjust to the new reality, but for people in an otherwise intolerable situation, it may persist indefinitely (witness the Cheshire Home residents). The leavers interviewed had been faced with major lifestyle adaptations both on entry and on quitting the military. The initiation programme for entrants had effected a separation between them and their young civilian counterparts, but, thereafter, some servicemen and women had maintained closer links with the civilian world than others.

Alan C., for instance: although he joined the RAF straight from school, his family had no particular military connections and when he went home – as he frequently did – it was to a small-town, middle-England setting with quite different preoccupations from those of the military community. Continuing to feel comfortable in civilian surroundings, when Alan married, he and his wife bought a house near to the station where he was serving and made friends among the local population. On posting, the house was sold but throughout his career he owned a property *somewhere* and he says that he 'always had friends off the station as well as on it'. Alan therefore never completely lost a civilian perspective even though it may have been diminished at times.

Stig, in contrast, did. Having had a less than perfect childhood, he embraced the military with wholehearted enthusiasm and severed his links with home and the foster families who had brought him up. During his years in the Army, he lived in barracks, socialised on camp or in the garrison towns and associated almost exclusively with soldiers. Returning to his home town 10 years later, he *had* lost a civilian perspective, and by his own admission has still not regained it. This is hardly surprising, when the Army gave him so much more emotional satisfaction than his previous, rootless experience of a childhood in care. But his lack of civilian contact for 10 years afforded him no opportunity to get to grips with civvy street as an adult. Small wonder that his return left him feeling stranded – and clinging to his identity as a soldier.

The pattern is repeated in other respondents and it may be seen also in our 'key' interviewees.

Jo Grant, Army wife and young mother, does not have to adapt to civilian life as such, but is finding it hard enough to adjust to civilian *status* on camp. From earliest childhood the Army has provided a framework for her life and joining up, for her, was 'like *growing* up'. On leaving she felt 'cast aside' and no matter how much voluntary community work she undertakes as a wife – 'it doesn't compare with being in'. She has no real frame of reference outside the Army and (coincidence or the attraction of like minds?) her husband is himself an 'Army brat'. Unlike Stig, on occasions during her service she lived in the local civilian community and she did – still does – have civilian acquaintances, though no lasting civilian friendships.

On the other hand Frank Warrell, the BT manager, was always, quietly, a free spirit. Coming from a family who were, if anything, anti-military, he never totally subscribed to the military ethos himself. Like many sailors, Frank settled his wife and family in their own home on the south coast and consequently, through them, he kept abreast of the aspirations, the gossip and the controversies of that community.

Angus Moorcroft, the vet, is interesting too. After a settled childhood in a family with strong naval connections, he went away to college for a while and lived independently as a student before ideas of joining the forces drew him back into a military milieu. Having waited and worked to achieve his ambition to fly, he did, for a number of years, immerse himself in the RAF. However, as he began to realise that flying would not satisfy him for ever and that his interest in animal behaviour was becoming steadily more absorbing and important to him, he actively sought out civilian contacts. He became a close friend of the local vet and, naturally enough, met *his* colleagues and friends. By the time he left to go to university, he had changed his self-image and was already, in imagination, a civilian, a vet. Angus is unusual in having set out to find civilian contacts, but he was very determined – much as he was when pursuing an earlier desire to fly.

This seems to indicate that, whether by chance or design, a

serviceman who is able to retain or to acquire a non-military perspective on life while serving, is equipping himself to fit into that perspective when he eventually becomes a civilian. Those, like Jo, whose *only* view of life is military and those, like Stig, whose *best* view of life is military, are very liable to hold on to their self-image as soldiers, sailors or airmen when they leave, even though they may still be young, even though they may have served for only a short time.

★ ★ ★

The active-service dimension of the institutionalisation issue is equally perplexing. Looking at the interviewees, it seems that, setting aside those who had had traumatising experiences of action, the remaining respondents with a large amount of operational service behind them, were, by and large, *less* emotionally dependent on the military than those lacking such experience.

Could this possibly mean that, although the military invests huge amounts of time and money into training and conditioning its members to perform military tasks 'for real', that the actual performance of the tasks begins to *undo* the conditioning? A strange proposition but one towards which the evidence of this small study points.

Certainly our two extreme examples – Alan C. and Stig – tend to bear this out. Alan, though never in battle, carried out or (in later years) directed flying operations in almost every major emergency from 1955 to 1984. Stig served in Northern Ireland and was caught up in the immediate aftermath of the Falklands War but always in a support role – part of 'the tail' rather than 'the teeth'. Among other interviewees, it was noticeable that the small number of respondents who had survived battle or who had been in *extremely* life-threatening situations, and had emerged unscathed, were now, almost to a man, surprisingly 'un-military' – in appearance, in bearing and in conversation.

Of our 'key' interviewees, only Frank Warrell had been under fire, but Angus had flown operationally during the Aden insurrection, Dave had been a member of potentially dangerous but actually uneventful foot patrols in Northern Ireland, and Jo, like Stig, had served with 'the tail' not 'the teeth'.

If it is the case that active service tends to decondition military men, why is this so? The beginnings of an answer may be suggested in the personal accounts of men who describe what it is like to be in battle:

On the ground:

> The minute we started leading our assault in, the machine-gun post saw us coming, and switched its fire on to us. . . . I began crawling forward on my own for about forty or fifty feet and remember feeling desperately scared. There were bullets flying everywhere – from James's platoon on my left, from the Argentinians ahead, and from my own guys behind, and the bullets were all ricocheting off the rocks. This is it, I thought. This is the end . . . Then I hurled [a grenade] into the air and it went straight into the machine-gun post and blew up.
>
> I took off and screamed at my men to follow me . . . I remember thinking at that moment that this was life on a knife edge. Amazing. Fantastic.[9]

At sea:

> As I was going aft . . . I turned and saw Russell had lost a forearm and was badly hurt in the other arm. Attwood and I assisted Russell down to the port 4-inch gundeck and as we reached it there was another violent explosion which seemed to be in the vicinity of B turret. I dropped to the deck, pulling Russell with me. After the splinters had stopped, I cut off two lengths of signal halyard, which were hanging loose, and put a clove hitch for a tourniquet around both of Russell's arms above the elbows . . . I went and told someone that I had left Russell sitting against the funnel casing, port side . . . and I went back to B turret to see what could be done.[10]

In the air:

> At that moment I felt a significant thump in the airframe somewhere behind me. I knew I had been hit . . . At my height and

speed there was no point in turning away...Painfully slowly, the altimeter crept up to a figure at which I knew I was safe. The next shock was more traumatic. As I levelled I saw the fuel gauges dropping . . . Experience of previous leaks and simulator training had conditioned me to expect a leak from one side only (afterwards I calculated I had received a very unlucky hit at the point where the two separate halves of the system combine) . . . I realised I was not going to make it. As if in a dream I watched the engine slowly wind down. In a silent, cosy glide down to 10,000 ft. (the cockpit suddenly became very warm), I had to force myself to accept the inevitability of ejection into the freezing Antarctic air.

At 10,000 ft. I pulled the handle . . . A large piece of the South Atlantic rose to meet me . . . and straight away I was off, being dragged by the strong wind on a wild roller- coaster ride from wave to wave.[11]

Images of confusion, fear and the nearness of death crowd each other . . . the noise, the destruction, the wounding and dying and leaving of people, the telescoping of time and the intensely personal nature of the exhilaration and the terror of combat. And this, perhaps is it. Military units practise and go to war as *teams*, but when the chips are down, when 'the whole bloody world is exploding'[12] each fighter lives through it *alone*. Under fire, the rules are bent or broken; everybody does what he can. In the words of a Falklands Royal Marine CO:

It truly is a shambles . . . and I found that my influence, once the actual battle had started, was minimal. And on the night, the battle was won by individual marines and lance corporals doing what they had trained and rehearsed to do as a basis, and their initiative on top of that . . .[13]

Thus conditioning inculcates habits of orderliness, of obedience, of trust and interdependence, but battle can break the mould. In situations of extreme danger each person takes charge of his or her own fate.

Moving down the scale from battle to operations such as peacekeeping, disaster relief and so forth, the same priorities apply though in a less dramatic environment. Nevertheless, there is still danger, and still the need and scope for people to act on their own initiative to ensure that the task is accomplished. However, moving back from the front line to the supporting teams, and from the emergency to routine service, there are many people in uniform who have but limited scope for individual initiative and little control over their own destinies. And not all of them are junior in rank.

We have arrived at the concept of autonomy. Military conditioning emphasises the pre-eminence of the group and no one in the military is absolutely autonomous, but certain types of work and certain situations give people a significant measure of personal control. It would appear that those individuals who have experienced a fair degree of autonomy during their military careers are more resistant to the institutionalising effect of rules, hierarchy, standardisation and the group mentality than those who have been closely supervised. It is not just a simple matter of commander and commanded or 'teeth' and 'tail'; some commanders constantly defer to their headquarters, and some juniors – even in tail-end support jobs – manage somehow to run their own show.

* * *

A degree of institutionalisation is normal for a serving man or woman in the armed forces, just as it is in a person who has dedicated him or herself to a religious life. To a lesser extent, some institutionalisation is also to be found in the semi-cloistered worlds of academe, medicine and the law. It is nothing to be ashamed of; it points up no innate deficiencies of character or ability, but it is a giant handicap when the guiding hand of the institution is removed. In this event, the individual who has had some control within the institution can assume responsibility for wider areas of his life quite easily. The individual who has not, has to learn, and this takes courage, practice, confidence and time.

CHAPTER 4

Leaving:
The Reason Why

It is astonishing how many people leave the military quietly, almost secretively, with no formal marking of their departure beyond the eventual receipt of a standard letter from the Ministry of Defence. As previously described, entry into the armed forces is celebrated collectively and elaborately as a ceremonial rebirth; by the same token, if leaving is symbolically a death, why are so many of the dead allowed to pass on, unburied and unmourned?

Part of the reason is probably that, given the choice, many people do elect to depart unobtrusively, keeping their inevitably mixed feelings and raw nerves to themselves. However, in retrospect, of all the interviewees whose departure *was* formally marked, not one regretted it. Indeed, on the whole, the more formal the leave-taking, the more helpful the individual found it.

Andy H.: 'Me and the lads went down the pub, had a few jars and they presented me with a diver's watch. Brilliant! See, I had to give mine back. It's the only job where you have to give your watch *back* when you retire.'

David E.: 'I was fortunate in having no say in the matter. There were two very formal dining-out nights and an informal party with wives. . . . Yes, I enjoyed them all; they were important to me in different ways . . .'

And where a leave-taking was bungled, the memory still hurts a little. Angus Moorcroft: 'It was a lunch in the Mess. They gave me a tankard bought from a fund I'd already subscribed to, and, you won't believe it, but where they'd had it engraved, they'd managed to spell my name wrong . . . When I pointed it out, they offered to get it put right – but I said no, not to bother.' However, he concluded: 'Even so, it was better than nothing.'

Nothing was what Anthony S. wanted. He went to some lengths to avoid a formal marking of his departure. He was leaving under pressure, amidst controversy, the subject of rumour and tittle-tattle. An indiscretion in his 'private' life had forced him to resign and he was endeavouring to stay in control of a host of fierce emotions – anger, resentment, sorrow, guilt, relief, anxiety. The last thing he wanted was to take his leave in public. He arranged a holiday to coincide with the last official dinner night of his service and repeatedly refused invitations to less formal gatherings. His wife explains:

> We couldn't see the point of going through the motions. The hypocrisy of it would have been appalling. To all intents and purposes they were kicking him out, hushing it up only made it more disgusting. Everybody knew anyway. We weren't going to go along with a hearts and flowers pantomime as well.

Understandable. But Anthony had given many years of his life to his Service. He had distinguished himself in operations around the world and had been rewarded with both decorations and promotion. His fall from grace came as a shock to his family and close friends, but part of the punishment which they inflicted on themselves was the closing of that chapter of their lives without a public affirmation of all that was good and useful in it. Anthony and his family found it extremely hard to cope with what had happened, to stay together and to rebuild their lives.

For part of what a leaving ceremony does is to provide a rite of passage into a new life. Not just an end, but of necessity a beginning too. The ghosts may not be laid but at least it is an attestation that that is what they now are – ghosts – problems from the past. Leaving the military without any kind of ritual ending denies the worth of the individual, and, in circumstances where the leaver departs reluctantly, it may exacerbate his or her natural tendency to avoid pain by not facing the reality of the end. It is an impoverishment in a system so heavily bound up with symbolism and ceremony.

★ ★ ★

Men and women leaving the military do so under one of four sets of circumstances. The first and most common situation is the end of a contract. This may occur when the individual is in his or her twenties in the case of a short service agreement, in his or her thirties or early forties if it is an extended agreement, and up to 55 if a full career has been completed.

The second situation is also quite common: the initiation by the individual of a premature ending to the contract. As with any contract, there is usually a penalty to be paid for failing to abide by all its provisions, and officers may compromise some of their entitlements to earned benefits while other ranks generally have to purchase their discharge. And, of course, if the departure is inconvenient for the military it will not proceed according to the applicant's preferred time-scale; in fact, it may not proceed at all.

If, however, the military needs to hasten the end of a contract the third situation comes into play – redundancy. Again, a penalty is paid for breaking the agreement and the redundant serviceman or woman is financially compensated.

The final and least common cause of departure is dismissal in one form or another. The military may deem a contract to be broken if a person is unable to perform his or her job – through illness or accident, through incompetence, unsuitability or criminality. An individual may consider that the military has broken the contract if it is possible to demonstrate unacceptable treatment – such as bullying or discrimination. Depending upon the precise circumstances, a few individuals are permitted to resign, effectively dismissing themselves.

It would seem that some of these situations would be likely to *create* unfinished business for the leaver, and interviewees were accordingly asked about the circumstances surrounding their departure. The assumption was that adjustment to civilian status would be easier where the individual had initiated his or her departure, where the cause of leaving was straightforward and not embarrassing nor difficult to explain, and where sufficient time had elapsed between the decision and its implementation to allow the leaver to think and plan ahead.

As usual, it became clear that the hypothesis was an over-simplification. The voluntary/compulsory divide between leavers was not helpful, since many a 'voluntary' decision was, in truth, nothing of the kind, with the subject feeling that he or she had been left with no alternative but to go. On the other hand, numbers of redundees and end-of-contract leavers with plans in their heads and money in their pockets were content to make the break. The more important factor here was the degree of *willingness* of the subject to leave; however, this was often difficult to discern. Many people had extremely mixed feelings at the time of their discharge and some were much better than others at clarifying them in retrospect. The 'routine'/'difficult' cause of leaving divide was similarly difficult to manage from an outside perspective. Individuals who had left the military amid controversy and as the subject of others' attention had been affected very differently by the experience. Some had grappled with anger, pain and embarrassment, while for others the predominant feeling had been one of intense relief.

Time was the clearest divider. Those who had had time to accept the reality of their leaving well before it happened, as opposed to those for whom leaving came as an unexpected shock. And even here, the distinction was not black and white since there were a number of subjects (Stig was one) who had avoided thinking about the impending termination of their contracts and to whom leaving came, perversely, as a shock. Nevertheless, taken as a whole, subjects who had known that their service was coming to an end at least 12 months in advance of their departure were generally better able to cope with the transition to civilian life than were people who had less

than this amount of time – *whatever the cause of their leaving*.
Two examples are Ian B.:

I went before a selection board in the June, as well prepared as I
was ever going to be and I thought I did well. I expected to pass . . .
They kept me hanging about for a decision, then it came through
in the September that I'd been turned down outright – no 'try
again later'. As I told you, there was nowhere to go in my trade, it
was as good as being given the boot. I could have stayed for a bit
but to be honest I couldn't bear it . . . I was bitterly disappointed –
and ashamed.

Ian, having unexpectedly failed to be accepted for officer training, immediately set in motion arrangements to purchase a
discharge.
Next Sandra J.:

When I joined up I suppose I was very naive. I'd been out with
boys but I hadn't ever been in love or anything. It came gradually,
the thought I might be gay . . . The blokes kind of insinuated it, I
mean, if you aren't a bimbo you must be a dyke . . . in the end it
didn't come as a surprise to me when I fell in love with a girl
friend . . . It wasn't her, but later there was another girl who was
'shopped' and some letters of mine were in her possession . . . I
was taken aback . . . sad . . . but I was tired of keeping up appearances anyway. For the first time, people were really understanding.
The provost guys couldn't have been more considerate.

Sandra left, supposedly 'under a cloud' but actually feeling
'free of a great burden'.
Ian initiated his own discharge, Sandra was administratively
dismissed; Ian left for the socially 'acceptable' reason of diminishing career prospects while Sandra was branded 'unsuitable'
and her private life was brought into the open. But Ian's disappointment came as a bolt from the blue whereas Sandra had
already become uneasy about her position long before it
became untenable. And in interview it was clear that Sandra's
homosexuality was less of an issue for her today than was Ian's

rejection for officer training. It was Ian who expressed resentment and a sense of injustice, Ian who was still existing in something of a vacuum – not comfortably a civilian, yet not a serviceman either.

These two examples point to an interesting distinction between disappointment (acute disappointment, that is) and disillusionment. The essence of extreme disappointment is its swiftness. Hopes and expectations that have been built up over a period of time come crashing down 'in one fell swoop'. Disappointment entails shock, loss and grief, and getting over it involves a process of healing and reorientation. Disillusionment, in contrast, is usually gradual and entails a painful acceptance of personal misjudgement and mistake. It is generally felt as a result of several events, and tackling it requires a re-examination of loyalties, commitments – even a whole life-direction. Disillusionment with a way of life is a fundamental issue and therefore, one might think, a difficult situation in which to leave the military. But this does not appear to be the case.

The reason for this may be that if one becomes disillusioned with a way of life, it is the *becoming* which is the most distressing part of the process. Once that way of life has reached an intolerable point, there is no peace of mind until the disillusionment is faced. Leaving, in this context, is the first step on the path to something different, and it may be hoped, something better.

On the other hand, for the leaver who goes feeling greatly disappointed, the most painful part of the process has only just begun. And it is alongside the realisation that a cherished ambition can never be fulfilled that the leaver has also to attempt the practical reorganisation of his or her life. It is, for most people, too much to accomplish at once. In consequence, disappointed leavers who *have* to concentrate on practicalities may delay confronting – may actually never confront – the issues surrounding their disappointment.

This accords well with the research we have noted which 'stages' the process of changing a social identity – confrontation, disengagement, resocialisation. Disillusionment may be exceedingly unpleasant but it does seem to contain within it the seeds of resolution. For one thing, it is handled by the individual at more or less his own pace and is therefore less likely to be blocked or denied. Thus the confrontation phase of adjustment will have occurred with the painful acknowledgement of disillusionment and the subject will have already begun to disengage by the time he or she is actually discharged.

The study emphatically reinforces the notion of adaptation as a process, with no short-cuts. It indicates, on occasions quite surprisingly, that however upsetting the cause of leaving may have been, the person who has had, or has given himself, time to come to terms with events before having to act, is more likely to make a satisfactory transition to civilian life than the person who has not had, or not given himself, such time.

* * *

At this point, let us consider three more case studies – all former officers. Oliver T. had plenty of time in which to contemplate his departure and was neither disillusioned nor disappointed but, in common with the majority, had reached the end of his contract and was broadly contented with his period in the Army. Nick P. also had time, but his experience in the RAF was extremely uncomfortable and he left a disillusioned man. Brian S. gave himself very little time, applying to retire prematurely following a severe but not uncommon kind of disappointment.

Oliver T. joined the Army on a university cadetship. After graduating he served on a short service contract with a Guards regiment and on completion of this, he left, aged 28, to begin a career in the City. Well-educated, well-connected, well-heeled, he moved on as he had planned. He found the Army 'tremendous fun' and 'a maturing experience . . . It gave me the kind of responsibility I'd have been given nowhere else – for men, equipment, decision-making, you name it . . . I had more immediate power at 25 than I've ever had since . . .' Oliver could have remained in the military but like others of his type, he maintains that part of his enjoyment and his enthusiastic commitment rested in the knowledge that it was a temporary arrangement. He gave the distinct impression that he viewed contemporaries aiming to stay for a full career as rather dull sorts who perhaps lacked the wherewithal to do anything else. Oliver today is the epitome of a City high-flyer and is typically bound up in his work almost to the point of obsession. His military years he describes as a kind of extension to his student days; he looks back on them with unqualified affection – and listening to him, one would conclude that they ended at least half a lifetime ago. Oliver is not yet 34.

Nick P. is not much older. He entered the RAF with 'A' levels soon after leaving school. Having grown up in a service family he had no doubts about his suitability for the life and although he could have gone into higher education he decided to try for direct entry to Cranwell and was successful. It was, however, a period when graduate entrants already well outnumbered non-graduates and Nick found himself in the company of men and women who were mostly older than himself and were more questioning of the organisation they had joined.

'To begin with I was a bit out of my depth and quite early on I realised I'd made a mistake not going to university . . .'

A particular friend had graduated in politics and Nick, who had never been interested before, began to enjoy participating in fierce discussion, arguing an ever more left-wing position. He was dismayed to find that although his burgeoning socialist views were tolerated by staff and fellow students, they were definitely not encouraged. After Cranwell, things were even harder for one of a dissenting disposition:

'To be seen reading *The Guardian* in the Mess provoked raised eyebrows and mutterings over the port . . .'

Gradually, Nick began to find the relentless pressure to conform stifling, and recognised that he would have to take stock of his political views and the importance to him of the values which informed them:

I doubted the strategic value of nuclear weapons, I didn't share the common paranoia about the Russian enemy and I hated the 'gung-ho' talk in the crew room . . . I was also uneasy at the amount of

money spent on defence and its relative lack of social usefulness . . .
the inter-service wrangling and the waste of resources . . . Against
that was the fact that I thoroughly enjoyed the responsibility and
the leadership . . . It's a powerful environment and, growing up in
it, I suppose it was all I knew . . . At times I did feel disloyal and for
a while I'd rein back a bit – but you can't keep your head down for
ever . . .

Nick's decision to leave the RAF prematurely was received fros-
tily by his seniors, his family and even his friends. He felt
extremely isolated as he served out his remaining time and
maintains that he was ostracised in all manner of overt and
covert ways. His wife Julie was 'a great support' through all this
but soon after he left the service to take up a place at university, the marriage foundered. The whole period leading up to and
immediately following his discharge was, he says, 'a complete
nightmare'.

Today, Nick is not a rich man nor is he entirely a happy one
but he does live a life full of ideas and activity. A college lecturer, he campaigns for his local Labour party and is an active
member of Amnesty International. He has remarried and is
struggling on a limited income to raise a family while continuing to pay maintenance for the daughter of his first marriage
whom, sadly, he never sees. Looking back at the higher standard of living, the security and the status he enjoyed as an
officer in the RAF, he sighs ruefully; there is no doubt that the
emotional and financial struggle has taken its toll. Nevertheless,
like Oliver, Nick speaks of his military experience as if it were a
very long time ago. Of his life now, he admits it is hard work but
it is motivated by 'determination, hope and a truer sense of
worth . . .'

Brian S. tells a far more common, far less dramatic story. He
left the military in his early forties, apparently voluntarily, but
in reality 'feeling I'd run out of scope'. An able man, Brian had
climbed the promotion ladder steadily and had amassed a range
of experience which would have equipped him well to serve in
a particular specialist post. He was never actually promised the
job but his seniors and contemporaries spoke as though it were

a foregone conclusion. Excited by the prospective challenge, Brian did as much as he could to prepare himself for it – he even learned another language. Then the post became vacant . . . and was immediately filled by someone else. A much older man, near the end of his career who, although senior to Brian, lacked relevant experience and 'didn't even want the job'.

Brian was devastated. It wasn't that his career was in ruins; he would almost certainly have been appointed to another post at a similar level. But it destroyed his belief in the integrity of the system. He was astonished when colleagues raised no objection to what had happened and was saddened when his swift application for premature retirement was accepted without any enquiry into what had occasioned it. Feeling horribly betrayed, Brian left the military for a managerial post in civilian life.

Today Brian is better off financially and possesses all the trappings of a successful man – an attractive cottage in a home counties village, a new BMW in the drive, a study full of electronic wizardry to facilitate occasional teleworking from home. Yet he does not appear to have moved far through the process of adaptation to a different social role. Ten years on, he still looks and sounds like a military man and still talks of his military experience as though it were yesterday.

His story was repeated, with permutations, by a lot of interviewees.[1] A crushing career disappointment, the sense of being cheated of a deserved position, the hasty exit. Some, like Brian, fell on their feet in material terms while others encountered difficulty in finding reasonable employment and accommodation. It seems, however, that irrespective of the material outcome, most of these leavers found it hard – and some, impossible – to relinquish their former identities, to become civilians and *enjoy* civilian life.

To be more precise, there was a pattern. Most of this group, like Brian S . . ., had established themselves in secure work and were living fairly comfortably. But, typically, they had not made civilian friends – had found that they simply did not encounter kindred spirits – and were lonely. They would talk about their jobs but not about their colleagues; their cars, houses, gardens and holidays but not about their social lives; not about having fun, not about sharing interests with new people. It was not that they were shy or that they failed to meet people but that they didn't seem to 'click' with new acquaintances so that friendship never blossomed. Why?

When asked, the usual reply ran along the lines that in their view, camaraderie as they knew it does not really exist in civilian life; that a leaver has to accept this and do without it. A sad assessment and one that any rugby club, operatic society or fund-raising group would hotly dispute. The truth is surely that these leavers do not feel they fit in because they are still, in their own minds, servicemen, looking for an environment which actually no longer exists for them.

It seems almost absurd that someone who has suffered sustained hostility, such as Nick P., should be better able to draw a line under his military service and move on, than someone like Brian S. who, at the end of the day suffered only a battered ego. Is it really because Nick was forced (through the intolerability of his circumstances) to finish his business with the military and in so doing, disengage and leave, while Brian was able to leave without having to tie up loose ends or distance himself from the organisation? It does indeed appear so.

★ ★ ★

Thus far we have compared severely disillusioning experiences with apparently less serious disappointments to illustrate the sometimes surprising finding that 'unfinished business' may be comparatively trivial and yet still block the process of adjustment to change. If we looked at a common and not too dire case of disillusionment and an uncommon, unfortunate tale of disappointment, would the same finding appear, even more clearly?

Frank Warrell, the BT manager, tells a fairly typical story of gradual, mild disillusionment. The first problem to set him wondering was the rank/social class/career prospects issue. Not having come from a service family and having little idea of how the Navy worked before he joined, he didn't understand how difficult it would be for a bright working-class lad to make his way up the organisational ladder to somewhere near the top. As related earlier, he achieved rapid promotion as a young man, but soon he began to realise that his career prospects were limited. He could not progress to 'proper' officer status – that is, the equivalent of the young men who had entered through Dartmouth – but could become only an SD Officer[2] with a usual promotion ceiling of Lieutenant-Commander. Frank admits that it is possible for lower-deck entrants to break through this 'glass ceiling' and achieve high rank but it happens rarely and only then, Frank maintains, by virtue of the social acceptability of candidates in addition to their professional capacity. Frank feels that he simply did not possess sufficient experience of middle-to-upper class modes of social behaviour to enable him to be at ease in the wardroom or to be accepted on equal terms by all its members:

> I've seen too many SD officers ridiculed by their own kind and patronised by other officers . . . I didn't want to be ashamed of my accent, I'm not interested in fine wines or stocks and shares . . . and my wife wanted nothing to do with any of it.

For Frank, there was dismay that fitting in socially was essential to success and a kind of annoyance that this hidden agenda should operate below the surface of what ought to be a meritocracy. In common with others, his dismay was increased when he witnessed dishonourable behaviour among that very officer class from which he was excluded. In Frank's case, the incident which struck him was not extraordinary. An accident occurred on board ship through the negligent handling of toxic chemicals; it was clear that blame would be apportioned and 'at least one head would roll'. The person actually responsible for the accident in Frank's judgement was 'an idle Sub-Lieutenant who wouldn't get off his butt to supervise the job'. In fact, it was the man's immediate superior (an SD officer) who, though ashore at the time, was called to account. Frank believes that natural justice demanded that either the man directly responsible for the incident should have been punished or that according to 'the buck stops here' principle, it should have been the Captain or the First Lieutenant who should have shouldered the blame. Instead, Frank believes, there was no compunction about 'dumping a middle man in the shit'. He was, he says, 'sickened'. Not so much because it had happened but because it had happened *in the Royal Navy*. In truth, the military has always had its share of scoundrels, bigots and self-seeking adventurers, but Frank, and several other respondents, were indignant when they perceived a blind eye being turned to shabby conduct perpetrated by officers who ought to have been upholding higher standards of honesty and decency.

Talking about it now, Frank shrugs his shoulders; it vindicates his decision to get out and try his luck in industry. He came to terms with disillusionment at his own pace and regards it as 'a blessing in disguise'. From his current perspective it certainly does not obscure all the good times he had in the Navy but it does make him confident in his belief that he was right to search for 'a better deal'.

Dan O. was dismissed by the military 13 years ago, for alleged incompetence. It was an administrative discharge since it was supposed to reflect no dishonour, only a demonstrable inability to do the job. Dan still finds it difficult to have to explain. He joined up from school, where he had shone on the sports field but had neglected his studies. His prowess in team games, however, eased his path as a junior officer and his early years in the military were taken up to a large extent with competitive sports. As he became older, he was posted to more responsible jobs and was expected to keep abreast of a deal of paperwork – which, through lack of experience, he found difficult. In his early thirties Dan fell foul of a new boss who was displeased with his slipshod work and was not inclined to allow others to help him out. Dan found himself subjected to a barrage of sarcastic criticism, in public, in front of his men. When he reacted angrily he was condemned as 'boorish'. Every mistake, major and minor – and some exceedingly trivial – was collected as evidence of his stupidity and incompetence and he received a formal warning that his work was unacceptable. He was, however, given no additional training and was expected to continue to participate in sports, though no longer now competing at high level. Dan admits that he was inefficient but considers that was not the real cause of his dismissal. 'I was always inefficient, on paper anyway. This was a clash of personalities and I was going to come off worst.' He did. When the axe fell, it was swift. He left the military reeling from shock, feeling cheated, used and lost.

Taking various jobs connected with sport, Dan has continued to have contact with forces and ex-forces people. He name-drops assiduously – senior officers, players who represent their service, coaches – and one would never guess, on casual acquaintance, the circumstances of his own departure from the military. But of course he hasn't left it; it left him. He is still hanging on, moving in the margins of service life, almost as though he is waiting for a second chance to prove himself.

The finding holds. Time is important. Time to think and to impose some control on the situation before needing to act.

Malcom W. is an interesting respondent in that he, unusually, had a generous amount of time between a disastrous event which spelled the end of his service career and his actual date of discharge. During that time he moved from shock and disappointment to depression and disillusionment and finally to acceptance – more or less – and a willingness to look forward.

Malcom was involved in a vehicle accident while taking part in an exercise. He was badly burned and his right arm which was severely injured, had eventually to be amputated. He spent many months in hospital and many more months based at home fighting to regain fitness and to obtain and use aids for everyday living. His worst moments were at home:

> I bent down to pick up Laura, my daughter. As I lifted her I over-balanced and we both fell headlong. There was nothing I could do to prevent it. I was so terribly upset – I felt completely useless.

In public he found it hard to go out and meet people. He felt 'unreal' wearing 'civvies' in the daytime, and was self-conscious about his artificial arm and his specially adapted car. After an initial flurry of welcome when he returned from hospital, Malcom felt steadily less at ease in the married quarters community where he lived. Everyone knew that he would be medically discharged once he had made as full a recovery as was possible: 'but it was like I was already gone, like I was dead, you know? Friends and neighbours dropped off, they stopped coming round . . . it was hurtful.'

In the end, despite problems with some of his skin grafts and continuing battles with bouts of pain, Malcom pressed for his discharge: 'I didn't feel I could get on with life until I was out . . .'

Once Malcom had left, he did find himself able to make plans and put them into operation. Today he is in part-time employment and spends the rest of his time at home with his children while his wife works, also part-time. He takes an active role in his local church where he is a lay reader and though it would be trite to imply that this life-shattering accident had a happy ending, Malcom insists he is not bitter or discontented with his lot. There is no reason to disbelieve him.

Part of Malcom's story is echoed by two wives of soldiers who have recently been made redundant. It is the part concerning being dropped by friends and neighbours. One of the women says: 'The rest of the regiment just acted as if the lads who'd got letters had been shot or something, and life had to go on regardless. It was horrible . . .'

Nevertheless, it was this painful treatment that was giving both women a focus for their anger and, through anger, a sense of control. Like Malcom's family these two redundees were guaranteed some time, and they were using this time to gather and vent their wrath, and so to disengage from the military more easily.

★ ★ ★

What has thus been discovered about the circumstances surrounding departure from the military? We have learned that the majority of leavers who depart routinely, at the end of a contract, are well warned of their impending departure and, on the whole, accept it. Of those who do not depart routinely but leave under circumstances of distress, we have found that it is easier to adapt to civilian life from a position of disillusionment than it is from disappointment.

It would seem that disillusionment by its very nature brings home to the sufferer an awareness that his or her associates are 'not like me'. Having faced this disjunction, the individual is then impelled to embark on a search for other, like-minded, friendly individuals and groups with whom to identify. Disappointment, on the other hand, cuts an individual off from his or her expected relationship with others 'like me'. Set adrift among folk with whom they perceive to have little in common, they may strive either to stay in contact with military or ex-military groups or may withdraw into themselves, feeling displaced and lonely.

Peter Marris in his work *Loss and Change* remarks that 'The will to adapt to change has to overcome an impulse to restore the past . . .'

When the pattern of life is disrupted:

> new purposes remain meaningless, until they can be referred to those which have gone before. This . . . is why the practical busyness of those who do not grieve seems hollow and unsound. They appear to have found new purposes but these have no roots . . . and represent a disintegration of identity more lastingly damaging than the painful retrieval of purpose from the wreck of dead hopes.[3]

Disillusionment allows for grief and a reconstruction of life's meaning; disappointment often does not. If disappointed leavers are given no time, or make no time to feel their loss, they may never overcome the 'impulse to restore the past'.

★ ★ ★

Which brings us full circle to the matter of formally marking an individual's departure from the military: an end and a beginning, a point of reflection, permission to grieve. Although many leavers elect to go unobtrusively, those interviewees who had no choice and 'missed out', invariably felt let down.

Jo Grant, Army wife:

> Nobody asked me if I wanted anything, there was no party, no present, nothing. I just left on a Friday at the end of work . . . Now you ask, perhaps it had something to do with being married to a

soldier and staying on camp. I wasn't too bothered at the time but I wish now I had something to remember.

Bill F.: 'I left from the MoD. I put on a farewell party with two other leavers. We split the cost between us . . . Yes, I would rather someone else had thrown a party for *me*.'

And John T. 'I had no formal leaving. Regrets? No . . . well, Yes . . . But it is *heavily uncool* to mind.'

A rite of passage is not always a pleasurable experience for its key participants. Our society with its concern for pleasure forgets this. We mark occasions nowadays with dinner or parties and make speeches – in the name of pleasure. It is this or nothing. But as service men and women are admitted formally and impersonally into the military, shouldn't their official leave-taking be similar in tone? Why can the establishment not devise a simple ceremony, perhaps at the lowering of the flag on their last day of service, to mark the departure of each and every one of its members? A brief, solemn, dignified moment to remind them to mourn before they attempt to change step.

CHAPTER 5

Leaving: Family Reactions

> When Robert was made redundant my world fell apart . . . He was a soldier when I met him and all our married life we lived on camp. I couldn't imagine him as anything different – or me. I took it as hard as he did . . . I kept wondering where *I'd* gone wrong, or if there was anything I should have done . . .

> I couldn't believe what I was hearing . . . I never thought of Gordon as a quitter . . . When we got engaged, I believed in him, absolutely. He was going to do great things . . . Well he didn't and that's about all there is to it.

Two reactions from the wives of former servicemen, different in tone, different in content but similar in the intensity of feeling expressed and also in the need to make sense of their situation by apportioning blame. Of course, not all wives are sorry to see their husbands leave the military but even those who believe it to be the right move, often find themselves reacting differently from their partners and feeling helpless, or inadequate, or downright cross as a result. And though this is hardly helpful to the leaver, family tension is undoubtedly an integral part of the process of preparing to leave.

As far as the study was concerned, the opinion of spouses

was not systematically canvassed. Respondents were asked if they could recall the attitude of their family towards their leaving and most were able to describe how it appeared at the time. In some instances, however, spouses were present during the interview and were invited to contribute from their own perspective. Furthermore, a few wives were interviewed independently and informal discussion also took place with a number of women who had been married to servicemen who were not part of the survey. In other words, contact was opportunistic – but it was interesting. A further point: there were no contributions from male spouses of former career servicewomen. As they form a very small group (though surely worthy of study in their own right) efforts were not made to seek them out and elicit their views. In consequence, what follows is largely comment from and about the relatives of the majority group – family *men* leaving the military.

★ ★ ★

Most men who join the military do so as young, single adults; most who leave are married, many of them with children. These 'new' people in their lives are not merely linked to the world of the military, they are part of it. They are familiar with camps and dockyards, messes and barracks, ID cards, road blocks, guards and guns. Wives are accustomed to the military impinging on their lives, their menfolk being on call all the time, and, if they are camp-followers, to moving from place to place, putting down roots anywhere or nowhere. They have a role and a place in the organisation, albeit it a subsidiary one to those in uniform. Some grow to love it, while others loathe it but for all of them, the institution of the military overarches their lives. Then, one day comes the realisation that it will end, not at some indefinable time in the distant future but soon, on a particular date, in a particular place. At that point the military connection, with all it has meant for the whole family, will be severed. It is, for most wives, and for camp-followers especially, a staggering thought.

Peering into an uncertain future, what is the nature of their impending loss? First and most obviously, they stand to lose the security of employment of the man of the household, with the regular pay packet which this brings. And as the nomadic lifestyle of many military families places severe limitations on a wife's career development, there may be little she can do to earn an income sufficient to tide the family over. It is a frightening prospect. Military salaries are fairly good, pension provision is sound, leave is generous, accommodation is obtainable, the use of a range of base facilities is extended to families and they are looked after, to a certain extent, in the event of the service-man's absence on active service, his illness or death. Without doubt, it is quite a package.

Another sobering thought is the prospect of losing the service community. Communities are centred on the operating bases – army camps, naval dockyards, RAF stations – with numerous families living in married quarters or in their own homes, close by. When detachments depart from the base, when the ships leave port, there are plenty of wives whose husbands have gone together, so in their absence there is a good deal of social meeting to pool resources and solve problems. In times of adversity, when the fighters or the peacekeepers are in danger, the community pulls together and there truly is a tangible sense of mutual support.[1]

However much or little families have relished the label 'wife of' or 'son' or 'daughter of' its withdrawal will be missed. For the unearned, unasked-for place in the military rank-and-status hierarchy is a passport to the peculiar, larger-than-life happenings that only a community can create. The parties, dinners and balls of an extravagance unthinkable for all but the wealthiest of individuals, take place with the backing and resources of a community. Solemn ceremonial occasions are made grand and are given meaning through the participation of people in number. The jolly, almost innocent air of festivity at open days and fêtes when the general public pours through the gates and is entertained . . . these and other communal events bestow a sense of identity and a feeling of privilege upon the families of servicemen, even though it may fade as life returns to humdrum normality. (For it has to be said that alongside its magic, the service community can also display all the vices of a suffocatingly small-minded, one-horse town, its daily business too often dominated by parochial squabbles and gossip. Close communities are not without their drawbacks.)

Together with their leaving of a particular base community, families also face the loss of a feeling of belonging to the wider society of the armed forces. Indeed, it may be its impending loss which awakens a consciousness of this bond. Suddenly, news items featuring members of other services evoke not a sense of rivalry but a wave of fellow-feeling; there is empathy with United Nations and NATO forces, while the civilian world lies outside. It is, in a way, like belonging to a large, varied (not always attractive) family with its own pressures to conform and its own extraordinary benefits. Leaving entails a divorce from this family and, whatever the circumstances, some pain, some regret, is unavoidable.

Strangely, however, many service wives seem not to have dwelt upon the consequences for themselves of their husband's departure – particularly if leaving was a matter of choice.

Marie S.:

> I didn't feel I could burden Graham with my worries . . . He came home one day and said 'That's it, I've put in my resignation' – well he *had* talked about it before so it wasn't a complete shock – but it was a *fait accompli*. Anyway it was going to happen, he was coming out of the Air Force and I simply had to get used to the idea. Though I was terribly upset . . . I don't remember ever saying how much.

Marie's husband had opted to leave the RAF prematurely having met a career block and being presented with a civilian job opportunity. Like many other wives, she was at pains to emphasise that the decision was entirely her husband's –she had exerted no pressure one way or the other. The application of pressure is clearly believed to be a cardinal sin. For a wife to stand between her husband and his loyalty to the service is considered an appalling breach of trust, moral blackmail. Therefore, it seems that serious decisions taken in the context of leaving the military tend to be made by husbands alone and that wives go along with them, lest they appear to be having undue influence.

But Dr Christopher Jessup, a lecturer at Bristol University, stresses:

> It isn't just the man who leaves the service, it's his whole family – and the break can be traumatic. Particularly for the wife, who may have given up a lot to support her husband and 'follow the flag'. She may, dare I say it, have become as institutionalised as any soldier.

On the face of it, this may sound absurd: 'as institutionalised as any soldier?' Wives are not put through an initiation, they are not trained to operate in teams, are not forced to follow the flag and may give or withhold their loyalty as they choose. How can they become *as* institutionalised as their husbands? Quite easily, in fact.

The woman who leaves her home and relatives to marry a military man and to adopt the nomadic life of service families does go through a kind of initiation and training, though informally. When newly married she is befriended by 'older hands' and guided in the ways of the community. The birth of children (for which there is immense peer pressure) will grant her full 'service wife' status, compensating for the curtailing of her freedom to belong to the civilian world of work. And when she is older, she will find re-entry into the world of work problematical. Like her husband, she will have become conditioned to operate as part of a specialised team – a service wives team.

Women who do not or cannot fit into this mould may be very lonely, as the following extracts from a letter to a wives' magazine reveals:

> I am a twenty-seven year old university graduate married for the past four years to a Sapper . . . After four years of observation I have come to the conclusion that unless you are: a) the mother of several children under eight, b) the mother of a new born baby, c) pregnant, d) trying to get pregnant, e) intending to have children sometime in the near future, the Army, both soldiers and wives, regard you as not one of them, and someone to avoid. . . .

The fact that [I] have no interest in childbearing/rearing excludes [me] from the only social outlets the Army provides. The wives' club, toddler groups and playschool are aimed solely at those interested in children. There is nothing for people whose lives do not revolve around them. The three years I spent studying for my degree involved seminars, lectures, group discussions and a general stimulation of the brain; after marriage I found myself in a society which discussed nothing but who was pregnant, whose husband had been promoted and the terrible colour of the carpets/curtains/decor in the new quarter. To say it was a culture shock would be an understatement. In four years . . . I have never met anyone like myself . . . Does the Army attract females who have no ambition in life but to reproduce?

I am rapidly giving up hope of intelligent life out there and am starting to wish my husband had been made redundant so that I could go home back to civvy street.[2]

A *cri de coeur* from a lively young woman who, in her own words, enjoys 'clothes, music, nightclubs, pubs, raves, holidays, reading, writing, poetry, literature and above all, working'. Marginalised within the service community, she must rely on the support of civilian colleagues, but it is an uneasy situation and one that will be difficult to sustain.

For the majority of service wives who 'follow the flag', motherhood will reduce their contact with civilian life and, correspondingly, intensify their involvement in the life of the military base. Their relationship with the military can then quite easily become one of practical dependence and personal powerlessness. Lack of contact with the outside world and lack of autonomy are, as we have seen, crucial factors in the institutionalising process; it should therefore come as no surprise to find that many wives are indeed *more institutionalised* than their husbands. The dismay of such women at the prospect of returning to a world that seems cold and unwelcoming is entirely understandable. That many marriages crack under the strain is understandable too.

★ ★ ★

Of our four key interviewees, three were married and all three maintained that the decision to leave the military had been entirely their own.

Frank Warrell acknowledged the influence of his wife in his decision not to seek officer status – and this in turn affected his career opportunities, leading him to buy himself out of the Navy. But this final decision was his alone. Angus Moorcroft's wife was not a prime mover in his determination to leave the RAF on completion of his contract and to study veterinary science – though he could not have done so without her support. Jo Grant's husband, Chris, was likewise the recipient of his spouse's decision to leave (and although he was not available for interview, it was interesting to hear Jo insist that she had made up her own mind; there had been no pressure from Chris. This suggests that acceptance of a spouse's primary loyalty to the service can extend to husbands as well as to wives).

It is striking how successfully the military has included families as 'associate members' of its organisation and how unquestioningly loyal most of them are. It is true that wives do not *have* to go along with this but it is equally clear that the penalty of non-conformity is an uncomfortable marginalisation. Thus most wives throw themselves into service life, accepting its not inconsiderable benefits but relinquishing a large measure of control over their own destinies. Small wonder that many feel utterly betrayed when the system or their husbands summarily put an end to a way of life which may have been difficult to adjust to in the first place, may have involved personal or career sacrifices, but which may in the end have given great satisfaction.

Susan M. is from Northern Ireland. She married Jim, an English soldier, and left her home in a small, tightly-knit rural community to accompany her husband while he served in England, and then Germany and Cyprus. Leaving home was a wrench and Sue took a long time to settle into Army life. She says, however, that everything 'fell into place' when her sons were born in Germany – 'after that it was plain sailing'. The boys grew up accustomed to moving house, flying in and out of Heathrow, attending different schools, making friends quickly.

It was a very different childhood from her own stricter, safer but narrower upbringing and she did have some reservations about it. Nevertheless, as a family they enjoyed the life and it was a blow when Jim's application to extend his Army service was refused.

'Curiously though', she explains 'it hit me harder than it did him'. It was not that she worried excessively about employment or money (Jim's employment prospects were good) but 'I was poleaxed by this terrible lost feeling'. Not altogether surprising. She had, after all, cut herself adrift from her Ulster roots and believed there was no going back; yet, having spent so much time overseas, England was in no sense home either. Jim, she thought, got over the shock of having to leave relatively easily and 'in some ways, he was actually looking forward to it – while for me, I was dreading it'.

Sue and Jim were sensible and they were lucky. Sue's depression was tackled by her GP, not with drugs but with the suggestion that they should seek marriage guidance counselling. They took the advice and were lucky that Relate was able to give them an appointment without delay. Managing only a couple of sessions before moving house, their luck held in meeting a counsellor who understood the situation and who encouraged them to begin talking it through openly.

Carrie is in her forties and her relationship with Stephen did not survive his exit from the Navy. Stephen 'came across as incredibly debonair and charming'. A little older than she, he was good-looking, well turned out and self-assured. He was also married, Carrie being his mistress. Stephen left the Navy as a middle-ranking officer, when his contract came to an end. He found other employment, changing his job several times but managing to maintain a fair standard of living. 'But the romance was gone', Carrie says, and furthermore, she feels it evaporated slowly but surely from the moment he told her he was leaving. Carrie, a well-off divorcee with a good job, a grown-up son and a stylish house, had seen the Navy from the outside only. She had been to occasional parties, had met his closest friends and frequently travelled – sometimes to faraway places – to spend time with him. She admits that she probably had an unreal view of the Navy but it was a view which sustained a stable and happy relationship with Stephen for several years.

As he prepared to leave the Service, Carrie maintains, he began to change. No longer dashing and carefree he became suddenly possessive, even to the point of proposing that he should leave his wife and children to move in with her. 'This was absolutely, certainly, not the Stephen I knew.' And yet, how much of the Stephen she knew was *him* and how much was an image? For the military image *is* glamorous:

> Ah, Malta, dear Malta . . . We had such fun. Parties, parties and more parties, heavenly young men in uniform – white naval uniform if you please – and it's quite irresistible isn't it?[3]

Joyce Grenfell, in gushing mood, making us smile at female susceptibility to dashing young fellows in uniform. Over the top? Perhaps, but there is no doubt that the mystique of the image, however insubstantial, is attractive. Admittedly, none of the wives encountered spoke in direct terms about their husband's losing prestige, nevertheless there were hints. Comments such as:

> He lost a certain – sense of fun – the ability to let his hair down – but then, we don't have evenings like we had in the Mess any more.

and:

> He's much gentler and quieter, more willing to compromise. That's been good. But he's definitely more of a slob. He's put on weight and he goes round sometimes in awful old clothes . . . I do miss seeing him in his uniform.

These and similar remarks express rather poignantly the feeling that men, once suave and worldly-wise, have been diminished for a while – out of uniform, out of command, out of their element.

★ ★ ★

Thus far we have focused on wives who, for one reason or another, found it hard to come to terms with their own separation from the military world. There is, however, another group who have struggled because they were well *ahead* of their husbands in the process of separation from the military. A high proportion of these women had never been completely at ease in a service community and greeted their husband's impending departure from it with great relief. In general terms, it appears that a 'civilianised' wife can be immensely helpful in both practical and emotional ways to a serviceman beginning his own 'civilianisation'. Even so, strains are inevitable.

Catherine, the wife of a former RAF officer:

> He is normally such a forceful, confident character but he went through a phase immediately prior to coming out when I can only say he was – timid. He couldn't seem to find the will to look ahead and go for it.

Catherine, a teacher, and quite at ease in a civilian environment, realised there would be employment and financial issues to tackle but was unprepared for emotional difficulties. In particular, she found her husband's fearfulness feeble, unmanly and even shocking. She frequently lost patience with him and she described how, during the rows which ensued, he would bluster excuses but do very little. Fortunately, as time went by and hesitant plans took shape, his confidence re-emerged. Meanwhile, the couple trod an anxious path for many months, wondering how their marriage could possibly survive.

Janice is the wife of a former Army sergeant. She works as the PA to the managing director of a medium-to-large company and is very comfortable in the world of business. She recalls being astonished at her reaction to her husband's joining the same world (as a junior manager) on leaving the military: 'He was encroaching on my territory.' She was irritated when he expressed opinions, based, she knew, on slender experience and was 'utterly infuriated' when he made comparisons between business and the Army, to the detriment of the former. It took this couple, too, a long time to settle into a new way of life, a new way of viewing each other, prolonged, Janice admits, by her resentment at her husband's acquisition of skills, knowledge and jargon that had previously been *her* province.

* * *

Unlike the adults in a family, the children of service parents have generally known no other way of life. For most of them the pattern of 'following the flag' – moving house, changing schools, making friends and leaving others – is unremarkable. It is what most of the children they know do too. And the upheaval which accompanies continual change is offset to a degree by the predictability of the military environment to which they are always loosely attached. Even children who have experienced a more settled lifestyle are still accustomed to the way in which their fathers' service dominates the activities, the plans and the whole ethos of the family. Despite having civilian friends and relatives, most children are unable to imagine how radically their father's leaving the military will affect them. The realisation occurs only in retrospect.

Talking to older children and young adults whose way of life changed from service to civilian was instructive. Again, it was not a part of the survey but opportunities to speak to children were taken as they occurred. In fact, although most of them had quite vivid memories of the time *after* their fathers left the military, very few could remember much about the period of anticipation beforehand.

One who can is Adam, whose father left the Navy when he was 10. He remembers feeling oddly excluded as his parents excitedly planned to return to the part of Yorkshire where they had both grown up. Adam and his brother had, naturally enough, visited the area to visit relatives but it didn't signify 'home' to them as it did to their parents.

> We were used to moving to a new place and all of us being – new. But this time we felt left out – or I did. I worried because Mum and Dad were so pleased . . .

Another, Jenny, remembers the shock of her father's discharge from the RAF when he had hoped – expected – to extend his service. She recalls the Christmas just before they moved out of their married quarter:

> It wasn't too good. There were huge money worries because Daddy hadn't got a job to go to. Not many presents. No turkey – we had chicken . . . And I remember we were given this moth-eaten synthetic tree by our next door neighbours, who had it in the loft; I suppose it was kind of them but . . .'

She readily went on to concede that it wasn't the lack of *things* that made what the family now calls 'the poor Christmas' so gloomy, but the all-pervading air of anxiety which the festive season accentuated rather than dispelled.

★ ★ ★

When interviewees were questioned about the response of their families to the prospect of their leaving the military, it was expected that the married participants would speak about their spouse's reactions while single people would describe the responses of their parents.

In the event, a surprising number of married men (though no married women) related tales of strong, adverse reactions from parents. Where leaving was a matter of choice, many parents had expressed anger at the decision, often claiming it was irresponsible and self-indulgent and, if the son had dependent children, a foolhardy risk to take. More than one respondent had become completely estranged from his parents as a result. Where the military was ending a son's term of service, many parents could not hide their disappointment and overtly or tacitly managed to convey a judgement that their son's career had been a flop.

The number of interviewees who recalled being upset by parental disapproval and the strength of feeling which came through their stories was revealing. It seems that the respondents themselves were often surprised at their parents' hostility (after all, they had been independent adults for a considerable time) and found it unexpectedly hard to deal with. It was clear that for many, lack of parental support was more than an annoyance; it hurt.

Andy H. (who was quoted in Chapter 4) :

> The folks came round in time but I could have done without their long faces and the constant 'Do you think you're doing right?' I was worried enough myself . . .'

Michael C. (the redundee) found telling his mother – who was so proud of her son's status as an Army officer – the hardest thing he had to do. Harder than telling his wife. It was so difficult to inflict this disappointment that he actively considered lying about it, but in the end he telephoned her from Germany with the news. And was she sympathetic? His wife says: 'She was speechless at first, then sad . . . Michael had to comfort her when what he needed was for her to say it didn't matter . . .'

John T. was one of those whose decision to leave the military estranged him from his parents. Having explained how his bid to gain parental esteem by following in his father's footsteps and entering Dartmouth gave him little personal satisfaction, he described, with studied detachment, his parents' reception of the news that he was to quit: 'I phoned my father and told him. There was a silence. He thought I was mad . . .'

Soon afterwards John received a stern letter from him saying how troubled his mother was, how unwise a plan they thought it to be, especially as he had a wife and small children to provide for, and trusted he would reconsider. Before replying to this letter, John contacted his sisters in the hope that one of them might be willing to act as an intermediary and explain the seriousness of his intent. To no avail; neither sister could understand his point of view: 'I felt totally unsupported.' His uncompromising reply to his father provoked further letters from both parents, full of bewilderment and fury. And then nothing. No further contact.

John has been able to understand this ferocious reaction by reflecting upon his parents' own childhood experiences and he has emerged feeling 'stronger by far'. He hopes that at some time in the future broken fences may be mended but is realistic in estimating the chances of a reconciliation as 'no better than 50-50'. John's objective, philosophical view of the situation has been hard-won. The emotional turmoil of the break with his parents and sisters certainly consumed much valuable concentration and energy which should have been channelled into getting a new job, a new home and a new start for his family. These things were slow in coming, and his wife's steadiness at this time was, he says 'amazing'. In retrospect, John regards the rift with his parents as a price worth paying for emotional freedom, but it was a high price and one which still causes him a certain sorrow.

Before we condemn these parental reactions as absurdly possessive, childish and counterproductive, we must stop and think. For they seem common enough to be deemed 'normal'. Let us look at the picture from their perspective. Most servicemen join the military as young, single adults, usually with the blessing of their parents. Their joining will have had an impact on the immediate family circle – grandparents, brothers, sisters and most of all, mother and father. They will have had to alter their perception of the young man – no longer a youth, a student, a drifter, however they saw him – to regard him first and foremost as a soldier, a sailor or an airman. A person in uniform, a servant of the Crown, acquiring with membership of the military, a particular dignity which he did not possess before. In reforming their view, close family members could not have been indifferent to the military. A large number of servicemen come from forces' families who are happy to see the tradition of service continued, but service or civilian, happy or horrified, the family will have been affected. Part of each individual's own identity will have shifted to become for instance 'soldier's sister' or 'father of an RAF pilot', 'brother of a Marine', and so forth. The idea will have been mulled over, brought into focus and incorporated. This, of course, applies to some extent when a family member joins *any* distinctive group, but it is very marked where that group stands apart from the mainstream of society, as the military does. Thus servicemen's families are, through them, linked to the peculiar world of the armed forces and whether they approve or not, it is a significant link.

The sense of loss which many a parent experiences on the departure of a son from the military is personal and may be acute. Many have been intensely proud:

> I had watched my father on parade at Plymouth Hoe for the King and Queen's Silver Jubilee in 1935. I had seen pictures of him commanding the Victory Parade in Bombay in 1945. As a Cranwell cadet . . . I remembered slow-marching up the steps at my own commissioning parade . . . I had seen Christopher command his own passing-out parade at Sandhurst, and now I was seeing Robert . . . I thought I would burst with paternal pride.[4]

Given all this, a son's leaving may seem like a rejection of their own values, their own judgement, a rejection of themselves.[5]

* * *

Families, too, have 'unfinished business' with the military. And families are frequently much more *angry* than the leavers themselves. Lacking any real control over the situation, *re*action is their only weapon. Reaction, then, tends to be strong and not always helpful to the leaver. It occurs at the point when the leaver most needs reassurance to face the future with confidence. Half-hearted support or none at all makes everyone miserable. Difficulties are usually resolved gradually as events take their course and family members come to accept their own regrets, their own losses. Only then can they begin to sustain the solid commitment to the future which they all need. Family dynamics are pursued further in a later chapter; suffice it to say that few experience an entirely smooth ride. In truth, Dr Jessup is right when he says: 'It isn't just the man who leaves the service, it's his whole family.'

CHAPTER 6

New Occupations:
In Quick or Slow Time?

Any discussion about the business of changing step from a service to a civilian way of life tends to focus at an early stage on the issue of finding new work. All too often success or failure is judged in terms of the speed with which suitable employment is obtained and the size of the new salary.

Individuals when relating their own experiences were themselves keen to create the impression of a virtually seamless progression from one career into another – and it often took some probing to reveal a fuller picture. The false starts, the half-baked schemes which never got off the ground, the rejections and the mistakes, these were hurriedly passed over. But were they unfortunate miscalculations, or invaluable experience? And is a rapid change really such a good idea?

It seems that the military professional finds it hard to embrace the notion of a gradual move, a slow change from a service to a civilian career. Most would claim that they had no choice anyway; that the practical imperatives of getting work, finding a home and creating a new sense of stability for a family made slow change impossible. Yet a lot of leavers did, in practice, have a break. An undemanding last tour of duty, a long vacation, a succession of jobs on leaving, these were common occurrences but they were not seen as part and parcel of the adjustment process. Instead, they were usually viewed as irrelevant to the main business of getting into a second career; unimportant happenings which distracted attention and delayed the attainment of a new equilibrium.

Perhaps it is not surprising that military minds think this way. After all, speed and decisiveness are key military virtues. Any move which smacks of hesitancy or irresolution is the very antithesis of the way in which a serviceman or woman is trained and expected to behave. It goes against the grain to 'make haste slowly'. This may be why leavers so readily viewed the experiences which bridged the gap between their service and a settled civilian occupation as having been impediments to progress, rather than as precious time which may or may not have been used to full advantage.

Of course, on exit, the practical issues of income, finance, housing and family stability have to be addressed as a priority – although most people will have planned for the *immediate* future before leaving. Nevertheless, to convert such temporary, provisional measures into permanent, secure arrangements as efficiently as possible seems to have been the overriding aim of a majority of leavers. Fair enough; but its supposed corollary, that time spent in any way other than directly furthering this aim, was time ill-spent, is surely questionable. It does not follow that the quickest route to relative security will produce the most satisfying way of life for the individual and the family in the long run.

Taking a break, or making the most of one when it occurs (as for many leavers it does), welcoming not denying it, using not wasting it, can pay solid dividends. But it is not an easy option. Far from denoting a lack of confidence or indecisiveness, it takes courage to hang on to a temporary, provisional lifestyle and to make a slow change.

* * *

Angus Moorcroft and his family lived a provisional lifestyle for many years. That this was planned and agreed in advance undoubtedly contained their anxieties during this time, but there was never any guarantee of ultimate success.

The last tour of his service saw Angus working for the local vet during his leave and studying for an 'A' level in biology. As he made applications for veterinary courses, the family practised living on what Jane could earn as a secretary and the equivalent of a student grant. They 'just about managed' and though finances were tight and Angus was already working hard, 'it felt', he says, 'very easy'.

Then followed six years of formal study, practical work and examinations. It took a great deal of effort from both Angus and Jane. The children, too, had to accept a fairly frugal existence. But Angus's commitment was strong. 'Indicators of change' seem to have appeared quite quickly. He grew a beard, wore his hair longer and dressed in hard-wearing, tweed and corduroy clothes, rapidly acquiring the image of an aspiring vet.

For Angus and Jane, however, their lowest point came at the end of all this, after his qualification. Angus took up his first job in a small town in rural East Anglia. As the most junior member of an established practice, he was expected to prove his worth by putting in more than his fair share of work; he had almost no free time, and, to make matters worse, was earning only a fraction of his former military salary. The standard of living which he was providing for his growing family was poor and the immediate outlook seemed pretty dismal. Furthermore, until that point, Angus and Jane had been surrounded by friends with whom they had had much in common, first in the RAF and then through the university. Now they felt isolated and dejected.

With considerable bravery, they decided that the only way things could improve for the family reasonably quickly would be if Angus could set up in practice on his own. It meant another sustained effort – this time to raise the necessary capital – and to do so Jane worked as a research assistant, while Angus put in many hours of overtime. Finally they raised the money, found premises in another town and after numerous tussles with planning permission, put up the nameplate. Like any new business its beginnings were uncertain. Jane did all the reception and administrative work and the children provided extra pairs of hands for routine chores. But they succeeded.

The customers came, the bills were paid, staff were employed, the reputation of the practice was established and the vet and his family finally found themselves in an unaccustomed role as pillars of the community. It had taken a long time but Angus and the family had truly changed step.

Once Angus Moorcroft had made the decision to attempt a career in veterinary medicine, a slow change was inevitable. The time spent at university and on practical work experience was a financial headache but it did give him ample opportunity to adjust to his chosen profession at a steady pace. The academic side of the course conferred a necessary level of skill and knowledge while field work placements gave him behavioural feedback, reinforcing his confidence. Unlike Angus, however, not everyone is in a position to pursue, or wishes to pursue, formal retraining. A less structured approach to change is more common.

Frank Warrell left the Navy in his thirties, feeling he could achieve better things but uncertain how to set about this. Before leaving he was entitled to resettlement advice and training but, like many others, he never pushed for the time off to attend.[1] However, through friends who had left before him, Frank was aware that it was not unusual for people to change jobs several times before finding a niche for themselves. With this in mind, he decided to take short-term employment immediately after discharge to allow him to get the feel of the job market before making serious applications.

Frank enrolled with an employment agency and for nearly a year accepted all manner of temporary work – a variety of office jobs, technical jobs and bookkeeping, plus some driving. The family was settled on the south coast and therefore did not have to undergo the upheavals of moving out of a married quarter and finding another home. This undoubtedly gave Frank some scope to ease his way into civvy street; even so, there were times when he and his family were seriously worried. Although he was never out of work, it was not easy, living with the lack of long-term security and he frequently drafted, then tore up applications for 'safe', routine jobs. It was an uncomfortable, uncertain time but in retrospect he believes that he learned a lot. Used to a fair amount of power and responsibility he was suddenly 'at the bottom of the heap, having to fit in'. An absence of responsibility felt strange but was also liberating, allowing him to observe the way things were done in different enterprises, to adjust his behaviour according to what seemed to be required, and to make mistakes while his profile was still low.

Two things in particular he says he learned. The first was that his customary military-style projection of self-confidence was coming across as *over*-confidence. He perceived that workmates thought him inclined to underestimate the difficulty or complexity of a task and were annoyed. And on occasions he thought that bosses may have felt threatened by his apparent self-assurance. Once he realised this, he was able to tone his behaviour down (and certainly nowadays he does present himself as being *quietly* confident).

The second lesson he considers that he learned at this time was the importance of tuning into the way in which different workforces demonstrate respect and deference to senior employees. In the Navy this was overt and standardised – standing to attention, saluting, addressing superiors as 'Sir' or 'Ma'am' – but within these bounds, working relationships could become quite relaxed. Civilian firms, Frank discovered, vary bewilderingly. At first he made the mistake of being too formal, only to fall into the opposite trap of believing that a culture of casual dress and first-name terms required a 'matey' approach to the boss. Having misread this one, he says he paid closer attention to the numerous, subtle ways in which seniority is acknowledged in different kinds of business, a valuable lesson.

In addition to making these sorts of adjustments Frank was also making contacts, and it was through one of these that he came to hear of a number of vacancies in British Telecom: junior posts in a possibly-to-be-privatised industry where Frank would be able to draw on both his technical and his administrative experience. He was successful in getting a job on a limited contract, and, despite the difficulties of working in a company subject to continual change and reorganisation, he impressed his employers, he stayed with them, and, moving sure-footedly from one situation to another, he progressed steadily to the level of upper-middle management. Frank still has ambitions, but altogether he is well pleased with the way things have worked out.

Jo Grant feels that she had no break between occupations, moving directly from a full-time job in the Army to full-time domesticity. She was already pregnant when she left the service and the camp where she and her husband Chris were living in quarters was not in an area where civilian work was plentiful. But, looking forward to becoming a mother, she expected to slip into the role of Army wife with no problem. She was wrong.

The tight structure of her working life disappeared. Chris would leave the house in the morning and the day would stretch before her. Housework took little time and, bored, she investigated adult education classes and voluntary work, but without success. The small number of educational courses available catered largely for men aiming to up-grade school-leaving qualifications and the even smaller number of recreational classes were full. The difficulty with on-base voluntary work was harder to define. Jo visited the HIVE,[2] the Thrift Shop and the coffee shop and was greeted politely – but she says she felt unable to relax in the company of the women there. It brought home to her how very used she had become to the particular style and banter of a male-oriented work-setting – and how much she missed it. The women, she thought 'were wary of me, knowing I was *in* the Army'. For her part, she still felt she belonged in uniform and she admits: 'I must have seemed rather arrogant . . . I didn't know how to play it.' Whatever the reason, she found it hard to mix with other wives and spent the remainder of her pregnancy 'getting huge and miserable'.

The birth of Jo's son and daughter set in train an extended period of 'baby-centred chaos'. Much of the time she was exhausted and a posting when the children were 11 months old didn't help. The packing, the cleaning of the quarter and the house move brought her to her lowest point since leaving the Army. Chris had gone on ahead of her and, feeling abandoned and vulnerable: 'I sat on the stairs with my head in my hands, and bawled.'

Soon after they moved, the twins celebrated their first birthdays and a new start in a new place made Jo feel more hopeful. This time when she tentatively approached the HIVE she didn't feel rebuffed (could it be that this time she approached with more of the outlook of a wife and mother, less of a servicewoman?) and she has since taken on responsibility for welcoming newcomers to her neighbourhood: 'It gets me out of the house and meeting people . . . I've made some good friends . . .'

Jo isn't aware of having changed her appearance or her manner very much since leaving, but she has probably adapted somewhat more than she thinks. Comfortable in jeans and jumpers she says she now has little need for 'posh clothes' and can't afford to buy them anyway. Her wardrobe is narrower rather than different; her short, curly hair is exactly the same. But if her appearance is pretty much unchanged, her manner seems to have altered a little. She retains the air of capability that she must have projected in the Army but she comes across as friendly and helpful, not at all arrogant or stand-offish as she feared she had seemed when she first left. Her conversation is full of references to babies and children and she clearly relishes her role as a mother. She also has numerous friends among the other wives and she is fairly sure they don't regard her as being different from themselves. However, none of her friends is ex-Army and Jo does feel, in a way, different. She says she has no regrets about leaving to have her children, but adds that one day, when they are older, she may consider applying to rejoin. In the meantime, she will follow the flag with Chris and 'do her bit' as an Army wife. Her goals for the future are not yet very focused, but with two-year-old twins that is hardly surprising. She has not set out to change step, though she has, perforce, changed a bit – perhaps enough to gain acceptance into her new circle without completely losing touch with the old. She is certainly not unhappy, but does not seem quite at ease with herself either.

It was difficult to piece together Dave Lock's account of the period following his discharge from the Army. However, it seems that he was helped to find accommodation in a London hostel where he was able to live on benefit while looking for work. He never did work officially; but unofficially, on the black economy, he took casual jobs for which he was paid in cash. It almost goes without saying that much of this work was of dubious legality, yet he did not get into in any trouble with the police at this time. In fact, he appears to have managed reasonably well at first and at one point was even able to move out of the hostel into a bedsit. Unfortunately, by then he had drifted, and continued to drift, into a twilight world of unemployment, debt, petty crime, drink and drugs, and he seems to have had no contacts outside that world. He had long since lost touch with his family and, having been dismissed from the Army, had no further help from that quarter either.

Eventually, having lost his accommodation through non-payment of rent, Dave moved out of London to a provincial city with a severe vagrancy problem and a vigorous sub-culture of the streets and hostels. Here began a seemingly endless cycle of homelessness, alcoholism and petty crime, followed by charges in the magistrates court. This would bring minor punishment and/or official help. Dave would then attempt to undergo detoxification – with varying degrees of success – and would live for a while under supervision. Sooner or later, he would relapse. Nothing has worked for long; he has not yet found the will to break the cycle. . . .

Of our four key interviewees, the most gradual change was experienced by Angus, with a long period of studenthood and practical training to prepare him for his new role in society. Frank planned an interval between his military career and his next move and though, in the event, it was an anxious, uncomfortable time, he believes in retrospect that it did serve as a kind of apprenticeship for civilian work. Jo had no gap between her military career and full-time domesticity as an Army wife, and discovered that her change of status and lifestyle was more fundamental and more difficult to manage than she had expected. Dave, disenchanted with life in general and Army life in particular, began to drift aimlessly almost as soon as he left the military.

★ ★ ★

The study reveals – perhaps surprisingly – that while it is by no means vital for a leaver to build a break into his or her plans between finishing military service and beginning something new, none of those who had consciously done so had regretted it. It also indicates that few people in practice move smoothly from one *modus operandi* to another (even Jo Grant, for instance, had some months between leaving the Army and becoming a mother) and that in many cases it is purely a matter of chance as to how productive this period of transition turns out to be.

Productive? How? What can be so beneficial about a painful experience of uncertainty which invariably places great strain on the individual and his or her whole family?

In a nutshell, a productive transition period is one which is *used* – to look back and to look forward. It is a time when the immediate pressure to achieve short-term goals is lifted and the individual 'freewheels' for a little while. The opportunity to freewheel may present itself during the final months of service, or, on leaving the military, or quite commonly, both. What is *un*common is a recognition of the importance of this time.

Transition is potentially a period of acceptance and healing, experimentation and planning. And not only for the leaver but, in equal measure, for the family too. Looking backwards there will be regrets and disappointments to come to terms with, a degree of institutionalisation to shake off and a harmonisation to work towards between family members with different reactions to what is happening. Looking forwards, there can be an acknowledgement of mixed emotions about the future, and an awareness of choices. The space to investigate choices can enable an individual to experiment, to dabble in this and that, to succeed here, to fail there. Failure is particularly useful, since, provided that it is experimental and not catastrophic, recovery from failure – knowing one can and one *has* recovered – can underpin confidence and give a person the courage to take calculated risks in pursuit of a chosen objective. Finally and most significantly, personal and family values can be reassessed and clarified during a period of transition; and a certainty of life's priorities is an invaluable light to guide tentative steps on a new path. None of this is easy, none of it comfortable but if accomplished – even partially – it can yield immense benefits both in terms of psychological well-being and in equipping the leaver for on-going practical planning.

* * *

If this sounds perilously close to psycho- babble, let us return to 'real life' and look in detail at two more case-studies, (of subjects previously mentioned separately in Chapters 1 and 4), one exemplifying change in slow time, the other in quick time.

Peter is a woodcarver. He is extremely skilled and highly regarded; indeed, a visitor to Hampton Court may see his repairs and replacements for the priceless Grinling Gibbons carvings there, fire-damaged in 1986. It has taken many years to achieve this, but not a lifetime, for Peter began his working life in the military. His story illustrates a gradual changing of direction, beginning well before he left his service and continuing for at least three or four years afterwards.

The son of an Army officer and the product of a nomadic childhood, Peter was sociable and friendly, had technical ability and was good with his hands. Like many service children, he decided on a forces career in his turn. The work he found interesting and the social life enjoyable, but, as time went by, he began to wonder whether he was, after all, suited for a full career. He found the restrictiveness of military discipline irksome and was prone to flouting the rules. This, together with his outspokenness and habitual lack of deference to his seniors, landed him in frequent, if minor, trouble. With maturity came a weariness of militarism and also a realisation that although others saw him as a cheerful extrovert there was another more solitary, more reflective side to his personality.

This quieter aspect was nourished by a growing interest in craftwork. Trying his hand at pottery, he rapidly displayed real flair, his manual dexterity and artistic imagination developing side by side. His wife Felicity (also ex-military) was keen on painting and together they began to talk about the possibility of working in the field of arts and crafts – some day.

'Some day' was turned into a particular day by an uncongenial posting. Now 30, Peter was given a desk job and, knowing it would be the first of many, decided categorically that office work was not for him. The job, however, was a specialist post and would have provided an ideal entrée into comparable work in civvy street. It would have been a much safer option than the one he eventually chose. But this was the point at which Peter was 'freewheeling', no longer striving to further his service career, weighing up possibilities, groping his way towards an evaluation of his abilities, his needs, his hopes and his responsibilities. Felicity, too, had an important voice in the decision-making. She had had enough of service life, was ready for a change and was prepared to give the 'some day' ideas a try.

Coolly looking the gift horse of his specialist post in the mouth, Peter decided that when his military contract expired he would endeavour to become a self-employed craftsman. Knowing that few potters were able to make a living from ceramics alone, he expanded his craftwork experimentally into other areas. With mixed results! But he eventually found in woodcarving a medium which not only excited him but also promised a reasonable commercial return – if he could get it right. Moving to the West Country for his last tour of duty, he sought the company of a local chandler and carver who made and restored ships' figureheads. Peter was impressed not only with the older man's skill and artistry but also with his down-to-earth, business-like approach to the important matter of earning a living. Understanding his customers, pricing carefully, working regular hours 'keeping at it', Peter admits he 'learned an enormous amount from his example'.

With nearly two years still to go before discharge, Peter and his wife decided that the way forward would be to run a craft centre, selling Peter's carving as its main feature. To the disbelief of some of their friends, who thought them crazy, they bought a farmhouse in the Yorkshire Dales and set about slowly equipping it to function both as a home and as a business. Furthermore, there was, Peter says, a definite suspicion from some of his colleagues that there must be something very odd about someone who could ditch the modern, macho world of advanced technology to pursue what they saw as 'arty-crafty, beads-and-sandals' ambitions. Undeterred, the end of Peter's military service saw Peter and Felicity take a short holiday (the last for a while) from whence they returned to Yorkshire to open the house as a craft centre. It was no quick and easy move into making a full-time living from what had previously been a hobby; the plot had been brewing for a long time – and this was only the beginning.

The centre held its own, just. Peter was still learning his craft, despite short courses, mostly 'by trial and error' and though his work was good, he was, by commercial standards, far too slow. His 'bread and butter' was nameboards but through an agent in Cornwall, he received ships' figurehead commissions and through a stand at the Yorkshire Show he made a name for himself carving and restoring figures for mechanical organs. As for the rest of the business, it was large-ly seasonal and for a couple of years, they struggled. 'We knew we could succeed', Peter says, 'but most enquiries came from the South . . . Eventually, we decided, over two bottles of wine, to move.'

If anything can be said to mark the end of the transition period for Peter and Felicity this decision was it. They had made mistakes but not irretrieveable ones; they had proved that their calculations were basically correct and that they could make their enterprise work. So, grasping the nettle, they moved to Hampshire, and Peter rented a workshop in a boatyard. While continuing to take a variety of commissions, he formed a link with Portsmouth Museum for whom he undertook occa-sional maritime restoration work. His flair for Gibbons-style carving brought him to the attention of the Victoria & Albert Museum and gradually established his reputation in the fine-art field. In parallel, Felicity developed her own skills in the paint-ing and gilding of some of Peter's pieces, a painstaking and often difficult process but providing precious help with major commissions, especially those for heraldic devices.

Nowadays Peter says he 'couldn't think of being anything else'; carving is his life. His customers and contacts have become his friends and they hail from all over the world. He sel-dom mentions his military background because he doesn't often think of it himself, though he still has a few friends and some fond memories from those days. But would he welcome the chance to go back? 'My worst nightmare!', he laughs, 'I like my independence.'

If Peter's story illustrates slow, steady, persistent progress, Brian's experience is quite the reverse. He changed step very quickly and quite decisively after failing to obtain a military post that he felt should rightly have been his.

Until the day when the devastating news came through that someone else had been appointed in his stead, Brian had not entertained serious thoughts of leaving the forces. When he did, it was with the knowledge that he was well qualified for a management role, if he could find something in his particular area of expertise. As luck would have it, a job was advertised in the national press which seemed tailor-made for him – even down to his recently-acquired competence in a new language. He made enquiries and attended a preliminary interview at which he was given to understand that if he could negotiate a speedy departure from the military, the job could be held for him. Feeling that his back was against the wall, he trusted to fate and went through with the negotiations. He was permitted to take voluntary retirement, his new employers were as good as their word, and in an extraordinarily short space of time he was out of uniform and into a pinstripe suit, working for a multinational company.

Brian's wife and two daughters were stunned. They had followed the flag, not always with good grace, they had made sacrifices, they had become part of the system and they had, latterly, enjoyed the fruits of Brian's comparative success. They could understand his bitter disappointment but found it hard to accept that he simply could *not* live with it. It was a traumatic time, borne, Brian's wife says, stoically, each family member working things out individually.

As Brian's new employment had been held for him, he was obliged to join the company as soon as he was free to do so. Furthermore, as he already possessed all the credentials they were looking for, there was no need for him to undergo any kind of formal training. 'I had a sort of on-the-job induction, which meant I was taken around to meet everyone and see the various operations first-hand.' Then it was in at the deep end. All was accomplished at breakneck speed but he seemed to have fallen on his feet. The job commanded a good salary including useful performance-related increments – and Brian was well able to perform. In truth, the work itself was not as much of a challenge as his former work in the military but he did have to set about building a personal reputation. His military background was known and, he says, 'I've made it work to my advantage . . . They accept that I don't like sloppiness . . . people not doing as they promise . . . I keep them up to the mark . . . They think I'm something of an eccentric [but] they deliver.'

Having entered the organisation at a senior level there was perhaps less requirement for Brian to imbibe the ethos of the company than for a more junior entrant. The impression is gained that he feels he has been accepted, respected and is also liked in the workplace, but that he does not think of himself as belonging, does not identify more than superficially with the company. He meets none of his colleagues or business associates socially and he is curiously detached when he describes his work. It stands in sharp contrast to the animated way in which he still talks about some of the posts he held in the military.

Moreover, looking at indicators of change, there are not many. Brian dresses smartly and formally, with short hair, shiny shoes, tidy briefcase and an almost excessive attention to detail. He does not appear to have developed a new circle of friends though his wife has, and as a couple their social contacts are now initiated by her. Leisure time is limited (as it was in the military) by the demands of the job and Brian's activities out of working hours are largely home-centred. So, no new developments on that score. The family's main difference in life-style has occurred as their income has risen, making possible more frequent holidays to a wider range of destinations. Brian has remained with his first employer and is not planning to move, although he does admit that the work is not always as varied or stimulating as he might wish.

Brian comes across as someone who has recently left the

military and is enjoying an enviable degree of material success. Only this is not an entirely accurate impression. Brian's departure from the military is *by no means* a recent event; it occurred 10 years ago, and, for him, the process of change seems to have stuck fast at a very early point. But is he content? Actually he is ambivalent. Pleased with his prosperous standard of living, he nevertheless responds to the concluding question of the interview by saying that yes, he *would* rejoin the military if it were possible on his own terms.

★ ★ ★

Peter and Brian represent two extremes, but if this study is anything to go by, there are many more 'Brians' than there are 'Peters'. So many 'Brians' leave the military with no idea of what they really want from a second career. Enough that they can find a job, get a house and, as quickly as possible, re-establish stability, security and routine. If the job turns out to pay well, so much the better. Hang on to it. But a great many respondents will, like Brian, admit they are under-using the skills and abilities which they possess, and, unlike Brian, many are not being paid anything approaching their former military salaries. So why do they opt out of the process of changing step so very rapidly? Why do they not use their early experiences of civilian life as stepping stones to better, more satisfying things?

There seem to be two reasons. The first harks back to the issue of institutionalisation. A large proportion of the survey's respondents displayed a continuing emotional attachment to their military past, from a mild to a marked extent (see Chapter 3). And this group of people produced none of the obvious 'slow changers'. Even allowing for the fact that the study is small, this does seem significant. It suggests that institutionalised leavers entering civilian occupations tend to seek, first and foremost, a replacement institution. To no avail, the military is unique. But for many, a weak institution, a partial protector, is preferable to 'going it alone'. Under the umbrella of the military, many interviewees had regularly taken risks that civilians would blanch at – were *able* to do so in the knowledge that the might of the organisation was always there should things go wrong. Once the umbrella was removed, however, risk took on a different complexion. It is not an exaggeration to say that for some, simply being out of the military was truly terrifying. 'More frightening than being on the streets of Northern Ireland. . . .', as one previously quoted interviewee put it.

It is perhaps not surprising that, once they were safely housed and reasonably well employed, many chose not to jeopardise their security in a starry-eyed quest for greater fulfilment. Hardly surprising either, that for many individuals their new protector failed miserably to measure up to the old one – one reason why they would talk so fondly and at such length about their service days.

Shaking off institutionalisation, taking one's life in one's own hands, is scaring. It takes time and a steady nerve. Sadly, few leavers believe *they* are institutionalised – 'other folk, yes, but me, no'. Yet, as we have seen, a degree of institutionalisation is necessary and normal in order to function properly within the military. It is absurdly unrealistic to expect anyone from such a background to jettison overnight his need for a 'higher authority' to refer to and rely on. Nevertheless, that is precisely what some leavers expect of themselves. When they find their anxiety hard to cope with, it is understandable that they should seek to put an end to it as soon as possible. Hence, it seems for many a premature decision to stop the process of changing step and to settle for what they have been able to achieve quickly.

A second factor seems also to be operating, and this has to do with the defining of aspirations. We have already seen that many respondents found it extremely difficult to pinpoint and explain the nature of their hopes and expectations when they joined the military. By the same token, many people leave the military without thinking seriously about their underlying sense of purpose and direction: the commitments that give their lives meaning, the areas of work that bring them satisfaction, the kinds of lifestyle that may offer them contentment. In short, what they *want*.

It appears that, encouraged by military resettlement advice (which concentrates heavily on providing practical, 'how to do it' information) most leavers approach the issue of rejoining civvy street as if it were simply a change of job they were making, not a fundamental change of life. As if the job *were* the change and not just a part of it.

But if a job has to be found anyway, what's the problem? The problem is that of putting the cart before the horse – indeed, of concentrating on the cart to the exclusion of the horse and thus, to extend the metaphor, to deprive the cart of its motivating energy. To ask oneself, 'What am I qualified for? What am I good at? What jobs might I realistically apply for?' is all very well, but for so many leavers this necessarily entails a lowering of sights in order to get started in civilian work. If the more profound questions have not been addressed, if the leaver has no sense of wanting to move in a specific direction, it is easy for him or her to believe that civvy street holds few opportunities. Hence many leavers seem readily to conclude that they have achieved what they can, when, in truth, all they have achieved is a start.

Work is a major source of personal identity and self-esteem, irrespective of what the job pays or what it demands. For someone who is loosing an identity, having an idea of the kind of work which would inspire the reconstruction process is invaluable. It may make no difference at all to that first job in civvy street, but it may make all the difference in the world to the light in which it is viewed. It may turn: 'It's all I can get' into 'It'll be good experience' – an end, into a means to an end. But this cannot happen if the leaver has no clear idea of what he or she hopes to make of this new phase of life.

Unfortunately, the study would seem to indicate that it is the rare individual who is possessed of such self-knowledge. This is no doubt true of the population at large, not just members or former members of the military. However, it may be particularly hard for servicemen and women to contemplate the meaning and direction of their lives. Military endeavour is essentially a practical business and introspection is not encouraged. Introspection is positively *discouraged* through the constantly reinforced training of individuals to act positively, quickly and always in the interests of the group.

Time to think, practice in self-awareness, practice in selfishness even, this what the leaver desperately needs. But few leavers acknowledge it, fewer still *demand* it, and of those who find they do have some time, most would not dream of using it in this way. This is why a move in slow time can be so useful. Travel, studenthood or short-term work experience is not only beneficial for the school or university leaver, it can give the crucial 'time out' that *anybody* in a state of transition requires. A period of conscious rethinking is not, as some people fear, a slippery slope towards aimless drifting. On the contrary, it is essential to the clarification of a sense of direction, which in itself is essential to the re-establishment of life's momentum.

Peter Marris in his influential work *Loss and Change* observes:

When novelty is consistent with our purposes, the change is substitution or improvement. Change as growth comes from imposing new purposes on circumstances whose meaning has not been disrupted.

He contrasts this with change as loss, which he says 'follows from the disintegration of a meaningful environment without any change of purpose . . .'[3] Thus a major life change without any significant change of purpose is destined to be hollow and ultimately unrewarding. New goals are vital to a new beginning.

CHAPTER 7

New Occupations: Traditional Routes or Unconventional Pathways?

It is all very well to conclude that new goals are vital for a new beginning. But most people have to work for a living and uppermost in a majority of minds are short-term practicalities – a job, a home, a structured life. Longer-term aims, if they emerge at all, tend to crystallise slowly. However, given the need for time, one may sensibly ask what kind of occupation is most conducive to the formation of new goals. Are goals more readily set by the leaver who follows a traditional route from the military into an allied occupation (uniformed civilian service, the defence industries or the security business, for example)[1], or is this task actually easier for those who strike out in an entirely new direction, into a completely unrelated field?

The question was one of the focal points of the study but, as related in Chapter 1, it proved to be a gigantic though fascinating red herring.

The issue is often debated by people approaching discharge, there being two schools of thought on the matter. One argues that moving into a career which traditionally employs former military personnel aids the adjustment process by virtue of its building on skills and knowledge that the individual already possesses. This facilitates a process of gradual, non-threatening change. With less to be learned before the leaver can operate effectively, confidence levels can remain high and the second career can be viewed as a logical progression from service life. New goals can similarly evolve logically. This school of thought would maintain that a move into an unrelated field risks demoralising failure through the need to learn too much, too quickly. And that lacking contact with colleagues from a similar background, the entrant into an 'unorthodox' occupation is deprived of much useful comradeship and assistance.

The opposing school argues that an allied profession as a second career may come to seem like a pale reflection of the military experience which preceded it. That continuing contact with numbers of ex-servicemen may undermine self-reliance and retard the process of adaptation to a different lifestyle. In these circumstances, goals may be inappropriately carried over from service life, inhibiting a renewal of purpose. When a change of step is made, the argument runs, the step should be substantial, setting new challenges and opening new horizons.

There is, of course, no doubt from a purely practical point of view that it is *much* easier to find employment in a related field. And an overwhelming majority of leavers do follow the footsteps of former servicemen and women into traditional areas of work. Mark Spilsbury of the Institute of Manpower Studies has examined data from the Labour Force Survey and the Services Employment Database[2] and he observes that the most striking fact to come through the analysis is the narrowness of the range of occupations which leavers enter 'considering the range they *come from* and the range they could *choose from*'.

Despite cuts and amalgamations there are still numerous trades in the Army, the Navy and the RAF. Yet on exit, other ranks tend to head for a very small sector of the job market. The uniformed civilian services and civilian security organisations between them absorb the bulk of non-officer leavers. Other large employers are local government departments and the Health Service. A significant proportion of individuals with more or less transferrable skills move into work as mechanics, electricians, administrative assistants and catering staff. Needless to say, many do not enter these occupations at an equivalent level (in terms either of salary or responsibility) to that which they attained in the military. In addition, a sizeable number of leavers find work as drivers, porters and manual labourers.

Officers, too, are clustered into a relatively few occupational groups. Jobs tend to be managerial. The defence industries which once employed a high number of leavers, now, as a result of 'drawdown', recruit fewer but opportunities in other areas have to some extent compensated for this. One such field has been health, where the restructuring of the service has brought a demand for tighter management at all levels, and where a number of former officers have found a niche. Other appointments which have traditionally been filled by ex-military officers continue to provide openings – for school and college bursars, golf and yacht club managers, in local government emergency planning departments, and in fundraising and administration for charitable trusts. Among younger leavers, central government recruits some, the police force some (though not many enter the other uniformed services) and the City some. For those with suitable experience, the aviation industry provides employment for a fair number of engineers, technicians and pilots and the security industry absorbs numbers of former soldiers. But again, the range is comparatively small 'if we bear in mind the breadth of occupations which exist in the services in which these individuals have previously worked and the breadth of occupations which actually exist in the civilian workforce'. (Mark Spilsbury)

The main reason why leavers enter such a narrow range of occupations is highlighted in a survey carried out by Simkin and Thompson entitled *Employment of Ex-service Personnel: the Employer View*. It clearly shows how one of the most effective ways of obtaining employment is by word of mouth. Where a line or personnel manager has been a member of the forces, he or she is understandably open to employing others, and organisations with a number of ex-service personnel satisfactorily working for them are demonstrably more inclined to view military experience as an asset. This does serve to reinforce the concentration and direction of leavers into certain jobs and industries.

A word of caution, however: it is sheer good sense for people coming out of the military to make a beeline for organisations where they know 'on the grape-vine' that they have a good chance of getting work. The Services Employment Network receives a useful amount of information regarding leavers' initial employment. A smaller number of individuals let them know if and when they move from a first job into a second and fewer still inform them of subsequent moves. Yet the longer-term data which they do have indicate that a significant number of leavers do not achieve 'settled employment' with their first employer. It is therefore probable that the small proportion of people leaving the military for 'unusual' jobs is somewhat increased in time, as leavers discover for themselves opportunities they were unaware of at their point of departure from the forces. That said, it does not substantially alter the conclusion that the overwhelming majority of former service personnel forge second careers with a small range of employers in a limited spectrum of the total job market.

* * *

Despite a large amount of anxiety as military numbers are steadily cut, it is the case, to date, that most leavers find other jobs. But the achievement of employment, even settled employment, is not the same as the achievement of *satisfying* employment – and civilian *work* is only a part of civilian *life*. Thus we return to the question of whether the admittedly smoother, safer passage from military service to an allied occupation is more likely in the long run to foster a contented adjustment to civilian life than is a disruptive and potentially difficult move into an unrelated second career.

Gavin aimed for the latter, aware of its attendant risks. He left the military as an NCO in his early thirties, eight years ago. Both he and his wife Penny had grown up in farming communities, and though they had achieved a far higher standard of living in the military than that enjoyed by family members still working on the land, they cherished an ambition to return to a rural way of life:

We wanted it for ourselves, yes, but the important thing was, we wanted the children to grow up in the country and be nearer their grandparents and cousins.

So they decided to move back to the area of the Cotswolds where they both had family ties. Ideally, Gavin would have liked to have worked a smallholding, but since, lacking the money, this was 'a complete non-starter', he had to come up with more realistic ideas. In the military he had worked in MT and possessed an impressive array of qualifications, from vehicle maintenance to HGV and PSV licences. But neither driving nor garage work was what he wanted for the future, save as a last resort. But what else? Agricultural labouring was out of the question, since, where jobs were available the pay was 'atrocious' and the work 'unreliable'. Penny was a hairdresser and was prepared to work part-time, but if they lived in the country, how easy would it be for her to find employment?

Looking around for a house to buy, gave them another idea. A pretty but rather dilapidated cottage for sale on the edge of a slightly 'touristy' village offered 'bed and breakfast' potential and also boasted a sufficiently large garden to allow for 'growing vegetables and keeping a few hens'. The drawback again was cash. Even in its rundown state, the house was priced close to their upper spending limit, and both it and the garden required much costly attention.

Nevertheless, they bought it. But to get a mortgage, Gavin had to take work which he hated, as a long-distance lorry driver. Moving in during a cold, wet winter with just the kitchen and one other downstairs room in a habitable state was, Penny says, 'a nightmare. Upstairs the roof leaked . . . The kids got colds all the time . . . Gavin was away . . . It was – oh, I don't want to think about it!'

For nearly three years Gavin was 'a truckie', driving goods vehicles to destinations all over Europe. It paid well and gave him time between jobs to work on the house and clear the garden. Penny, meanwhile, built up a hairdressing clientele in the village, chiefly comprising elderly people and young families whom she visited in their homes. She was not able to charge much but it was largely her efforts which established the family in the village – an invaluable first step. Meanwhile, the cottage was taking longer and costing more than either Penny or Gavin had anticipated, and they were often intensely dispirited: 'If cutting our losses would have got us anywhere, we might have done it, but we had committed ourselves and there was no way back', Penny remembers. In any case, there was no doubt in either of their minds about wanting a rural lifestyle, the problem was how to achieve it as a family unit. Gavin's earnings were going largely into renovating the property to a standard that would attract paying guests. It was taking 'forever" and putting great strain on the whole family. Gavin meanwhile loathed his job and resented being unable to share village life and contact with their wider family which Penny and the children enjoyed. There were rows, sulks and silences.

And then a friendly neighbour casually brought to Gavin's attention a course at the local college of further education. As Gavin had been working on the house and garden between long-haul jobs, he had gained quite a reputation for himself as a DIY expert. In particular, he had became known in the village for his ability to mend broken equipment such as lawnmowers, strimmers and sanders, and he found himself repairing things as favours, occasionally receiving small sums of cash or amounts of produce in return. The course in question taught the operation, maintenance and repair of farm and forestry machinery; he was immediately interested. With his experience as a motor mechanic, his hope was that with this extra course under his belt, he could seek work with one of a small number of agricultural employers in the area. It was a gamble but, he says: 'I was determined to give it my best shot.'

During the course, Gavin made strenuous efforts to further his chances of employment, and it was through contacts made at this time that he eventually was able to rent space at a garden centre where he set up a garden machinery repair workshop. A small business, precarious at first and still 'a perpetual headache', but it became, and remains, profitable. Penny continues to work as a hairdresser in the village. The cottage, though comfortable, is far from achieving its picture-postcard potential. There are no bed and breakfast guests, no hens in the coop, and only a few vegetables in the garden – but Gavin and Penny feel confident that the worst is behind them. Penny: 'We're living where we want to be and we're giving our children the best start . . . It's been worth all the hard work.' And Gavin: 'Now I'm established, I can truthfully say I'm pleased with myself. Very pleased.'

Goals for the future? To bring the family's disposable income back up to what it was in the military, but this time with all the advantages of a lifestyle which they prize – and, keen to elaborate, Gavin launches into a torrent of ideas and explanations, diving into drawers to find relevant pieces of paper.

Gavin and Penny's dream of country living sustained them through quite considerable hardship, and the achievement of eventual success has predictably afforded them great satisfaction.

At first glance, the study appears to provide an unequivocal answer to our question: unconventional pathways – such as the one taken by Gavin and Penny – seem more likely to nourish productive change than traditional routes. About one-fifth of respondents considered themselves well satisfied with their lives now, identified strongly with their current civilian role in society and did not find the notion of returning to a military way of life at all tempting. Their assertions were supported by substantial 'indicators of change' in both material terms (a change of attachment manifested in lifestyle, appearance, manner and social networks) and attitudinal terms (enthusiasm for the new way of life, realistic goals and an easy relationship with the past). These people can therefore be viewed as the survey's most successful adapters to civilian status. And a large majority of them – around three-quarters – had taken a major step away from the military environment into non-traditional second careers.

QED? Well, not entirely. Apart from the statistical difficulties of a small study[3] which render the drawing of absolute conclusions unwise, one cannot ignore the patently successful adjustment of around one-quarter of the subjects in this group, who moved into, and now identify strongly with, traditional areas of work. Nevertheless, it is interesting that the figures are this way around: that those who attempt a radical transformation of their lives apparently stand such a good chance of long-term contentment. Especially since the value of 'making haste slowly' has been demonstrated. Are we saying now that a major change of direction, with all the upheaval it will inevitably bring, may be a good idea? Is that not somewhat contradictory? Actually it is not, for we are not questioning the matter of *speed* of change and we *are* now talking about the next phase in the adjustment process. For while at the heart of the question 'in quick or slow time?' lies the matter of the accomplishment of 'disengagement' from the military, at the heart of the question 'traditional routes or unconventional pathways?' lies the issue of 'resocialisation'.

The individual having now disengaged to some degree, our puzzle really turns on why it should *appear* to be more effective to attempt resocialisation into a *very* different social role than resocialisation into a *slightly* different one.

So what is resocialisation and what are the factors which influence its accomplishment? Resocialisation is the assumption of a new role in society; it is being regarded differently, both by others and also by oneself. Successful resocialisation will result in the individual's feeling not only capable and confident in a new endeavour, but also feeling suitably and gainfully employed in what is, for him or her, a worthwhile undertaking. To define a worthwhile use of working time one cannot employ standardised judgements about the moral or financial value of the job. The worth of an occupation will not be the same in one person's estimation as it is in another's. But for anyone, a worthwhile job will reflect his own priorities and allow him to pursue what he considers to be important ends. If what someone *does* with his working life is congruent in this way with what he *is* – his values and his objectives – it becomes possible for him to construct an increasingly secure new persona as time passes and experience accumulates. A dissonance, such as results from undertaking work which is personally unrewarding, will encourage the individual to cling to his old persona (as did the prisoners and the severely disabled in the studies described in Chapter 3) in order to maintain a self-image with which he feels comfortable.

The survey supports previous research in finding that the single most important factor in the resocialisation process is the will to do it. It seems that people will not resocialise unless they really want to. In negotiating a major life change, many will take the most conservative option open to them, since change is frightening. For ex-servicemen and women, this usually means a move into a traditional occupation, using skills and knowledge they acquired in the forces and providing continuing contact with others from a similar background. The worth of the occupation itself (in terms of congruency with personal values) is not often a primary consideration. But where it is, the will to resocialise is found to be every bit as strong in leavers who opt for a traditional second career as it is in the less conventional group.

There is undoubtedly a significant proportion of leavers finding real fulfilment, straightforwardly, in occupations which have much in common with service life.

Derek, for example: Derek left the Army in his late twenties and, with the help of a Service employment agency, was recruited into the Prison Service. It was his first job as a civilian (having joined the Army straight from school) and he went into it with an open mind. He had enjoyed military service in an infantry regiment, but by the time he left he had had enough of the continual moves and detachments which caused family upheaval and too often separated him from his wife and two young children. The prison service was attractive first because: 'It was available.' Furthermore 'It was regular work, regular pay . . . there was accommodation provided . . . the uniform and the discipline appealed . . . I could see myself doing it.' Though, he admits, he had very little idea what the job really entailed. 'I'd seen *Porridge* on the telly, that's all.'

After a brief period of training he took up his first post, 'not very much the wiser', but he loved it. 'Right from the start I knew I'd found my niche, so to speak.' He discovered he was readily able to empathise with most of the prisoners in his charge, without becoming emotionally involved in their problems. And, far from finding a prison an oppressive place of work, he says: 'There's a lot of humour . . . and friendly rivalry . . . It's tough because it's meant to be, but there's caring as well . . .'

Ten years on, Derek has moved establishments on promotion and has developed an expertise with disturbed and difficult prisoners. He is in line for further advancement and he is eager to progress. Looking back, he says it was 'tremendous good luck' that he entered the Prison Service, where he feels he has been able to develop his potential more fully than would have been possible had he remained in the Army.

A similar story is told by Sue, also a former soldier, now a policewoman. She moved straight from the Army into the police force seven years ago and is enjoying in her police role many of the things she sought but only partially found in the Army. 'Excitement – and doing a job that really matters', for instance. In the military, Sue was involved in office administration and while she was 'no danger-freak' she was slightly disappointed at the unexpectedly safe, routine nature of her Army career.

'Police work is as boring as any other job 90 per cent of the time', she explains, 'but that other 10 per cent is the real thing.' Equality is another issue: 'The police isn't equal. In every force a woman has to be head and shoulders above the men to get anywhere . . . but if you ask me, the atmosphere for women is 10 times better than in the military. In the police, if you're good, there's at least a fighting chance you might be taken seriously . . .' One woman's opinion. But Sue is now a serious 'career' police officer who identifies wholeheartedly with her new way of life. She, like Derek, has been promoted, and she too is hoping for further advancement in the future.

* * *

The respondents in the survey who had taken unusual career paths had mostly done so from a conviction that their particular choice would provide a quality of life that they greatly desired. It is not surprising that most had thought very carefully before embarking upon difficult and possibly risky ventures, nor that, once under way, their commitment was strong enough to withstand inevitable anxieties, setbacks and changes of plan.

But the case histories illustrate the finding that intrinsically it is neither easier nor harder to make the adjustment from service to civilian life in one *kind* of occupation as opposed to another. It is not the occupation itself that makes the difference, but the *wanting* it. The lower-risk option of entering an allied occupation may often be (but is not invariably) accompanied by a weaker commitment to change. But again, it is not the nature of the second career which is crucial but the sincerity of the individual's attachment to it.

Motivation, therefore, is all. The way in which very strong motivation can propel an individual through the confrontation, disengagement and then resocialisation phases of the changing process is most clearly demonstrated in subjects whose sanity has depended upon an ability to change or whose convictions have demanded it. Only a small number of military leavers interviewed were in this position, so a brief look at other people's research at this point may be illuminating.

★ ★ ★

Pat Howes conducted a series of interviews with gay men who had felt compelled to 'come out' in order to preserve their mental balance.[4] They had, in consequence, declared their homosexuality and sought the company of other homosexuals.

All the interviewees talked about a painful period – usually in late adolescence – when they realised they were not heterosexual, suspected they were gay but did not know what to do nor whom to confide in. This was often followed by a difficult time of vacillation between rejection and acceptance, first of their own homosexuality and then of membership of their local gay community as they gradually increased their involvement with it. Finally, if and when they found friendship and a kind of security in homosexual company, they were able to come to comfortable terms with 'straight' society. Interestingly, for many people this entailed little or no outward change in their everyday manner or appearance but 'coming out' simply gave them a confidence they had hitherto lacked:

I'm gay and that's that. If people don't like it, that's just too bad. But it's not something I feel is an issue. A lot of people know about me at work. Some have asked me if I'm gay and I've said 'Yes'. Often they don't believe it because I don't look effeminate.

What struck Pat Howes most forcibly was that despite many problems and a certain amount of unhappiness, not one of the interviewees expressed any regret. By declaring their homosexuality they felt they were being true to themselves and changing their identity from the confused and uncertain to the positive if difficult status of the homosexual: 'It was like taking a step . . . like getting married. There was no turning back. I didn't want to turn back.'

Between 1990 and 1994 nearly 300 individuals, around 50 of them women, were administratively dismissed from the military for homosexuality. Several have made public statements and they range from bitter, angry sentiments such as those from a sailor who was discovered completely by chance, so discreet had he been, to the bewilderment of a man who had declared his homosexual tendencies but at the same time had voiced his personal and religious commitment to celibacy. For many, like Sandra – whom we have already met in Chapter 4 – discovery was a relief.

Sandra says that her sexuality never caused her personal anguish. She was relatively mature when she embarked upon her first relationship with another woman and felt no guilt or sorrow about it. In time she told her family, but she did not tell the military. Why not? She had no desire to lose her job, her way of life or her friends and, at first, saw no reason why she *should*. However, the strain of a double life weighed heavily on her and at times she was extremely unhappy. A turning point for Sandra came when a young male friend with whom she had contact at work introduced her to the Lesbian and Gay Christian Movement. Here she found immediate acceptance and here she says she began to gather the emotional strength for what she knew in the long run was inevitable – either she would be 'outed' by the military or she would feel compelled to 'come out' under her own volition.

When she was discovered she did regret that things had happened that way : 'I'd got to the point where I was almost strong enough to take the initiative myself but – there it is . . .' As it was, she was pleased that the secrecy was over and was moved by the amount of support she received from numerous friends, gay and straight, Christians and non-believers. The moment she had dreaded was 'not so terrible after all.'

Sandra went to college on leaving the forces and worked hard to gain an HNC diploma. Thereafter she found employment in pharmaceutical research; moreover, at college she met the young woman who has since become her permanent partner. For her, new goals have proceeded from the liberating effect of being able to live and work without deceit. Her change of career has been part of a radical new start and her resocialisation has been driven by an inner need to see it through. So relaxed and positive is she nowadays, one would never suspect that her life had once been so complicated.

A change in self-perception and in the way in which others perceive one also occurs dramatically where forces of conviction come into play. Another piece of work by Pat Howes is a survey entitled 'Becoming a Parson: Change of Life-plan and the voice of God'.[5] In this, 12 late entrants to the Anglican ministry were questioned about their change of direction in middle age. None of the men had experienced any kind of sudden conversion, all had had a background of religious commitment over many years and felt themselves to be responding to a desire, a call, which in most cases appeared gradually but would not be ignored. In this respect, the group were similar to the homosexuals. All of them had to accept losses when they were ordained (financial losses, some loss of friends, loss of domestic privacy as they set up home in a clergy house and not infrequently, loss of marital harmony, at least for a while) but the decision was not actually about weighing up these losses against possible gains but about whether or not to move towards a truer expression of the way in which they saw themselves and the way in which they wanted to live their lives.

Again, like for the homosexuals, there was struggle:

It was quite a battle I was having with myself. I'd gone through the stage when I was sure I wanted to go in and come to a phase when

I didn't want to go in . . . I was getting more and more money in my job. I'd a good future in front of me in many respects and we'd now got a family and a house. But there was a constant niggling in the mind that would never go, regardless of what I did.

And great relief when the decision was finally made:

> . . . now I can do what I've always wanted to do. This is something I really enjoy . . . I feel I am at last doing something that really matters.

Geoff, a former RAF officer, tells a similar story. A churchgoer from his youth, he had nevertheless no thoughts of pursuing a leadership role of any kind – until, in early middle age: 'I got the church as a secondary duty.' (It was his responsibility to oversee the administration of the station church, to ensure that the fabric of the building was maintained, to attend services and, occasionally, to lead prayers.)

He felt surprisingly comfortable in this work, and in due course asked for some extra, more theologically-based, training. Recommendations, selection boards and the granting of permission from the RAF followed with comparative ease, and he was given a place on the Non-Stipendary Ministers Course at St. Stephen's House in Oxford. It was a demanding course, not least because it had to be undertaken alongside his RAF service, and one which tested his growing resolve to become a 'worker priest'.

But then, at the end of his course, he hit opposition. The RAF would not allow his ordination. He could take up the office of Reader but could not operate as a worker priest in the military. Their reasons for refusing were not spelled out clearly. There was a moral difficulty with having a clergyman in a combat role and there was an executive difficulty in having him in a position to give military orders. There was also a 'good order and discipline' difficulty in opening up the possibility of having worker priests who might not be of commissioned rank. It had all the makings of a fascinating debate, but at the end of the day, it was not debated – Geoff's request was simply refused.

Geoff says he was 'disappointed' – an understatement. Even so, he accepted the decision: 'The military came first until the moment I left.'

He had obviously impressed his course tutors, however, and it was made known to him that should he, at some point, be free to leave the RAF, the Church would consider him for the full-time ministry.

So it was that, in the latter stage of a service career, Geoff voluntarily left the military to begin an entirely new life as a priest. The enormity of this step never seriously crossed his mind. (In fact, so sure was he then, and so sure does he remain, that in interview he was quite puzzled to be asked about the doubts he might reasonably have entertained before making such a move.) For, at an age and seniority when he could have confidently expected agreeable postings in the RAF, he traded these in for more training, little money, and a new kind of responsibility for which he felt alarmingly inadequate. Highly institutionalised (he had entered the military as a boy apprentice), he struggled to learn the ropes both as a civilian and as a curate – and it was, he admits: 'a very difficult time'. Yet not once did he regret his decision. Looking back, he is in some ways grateful he failed in his aim to become a worker priest, since the years he spent instead in a rural parish and now in semi-retirement, have been personally fulfilling, challenging and, in his own estimation, happy.

Clearly, motivation this strong *drives* the process of social role change forward to a conclusion. It enables such individuals as Geoff to let go of the past and to identify fully with the present – because for them, it is only within the context of the present that they are able to form coherent aspirations for the future.

★ ★ ★

Having established that anyone who is determined to change can and probably will do so, the study does suggest that some factors operating in the workplace can help or hinder the process. The most significant of these is the amount and complexity of learning required to become effective in the new occupation.

While the taking up of any new job entails a period of reorientation and adjustment, it seems that the accomplishment of a major life change demands a more profound intellectual investment. Interviewees such as Angus Moorcroft, who underwent a long period of formal study, made that investment as a matter of course but it is interesting to note that the 'highly successful adapters' in traditional occupations have also sought out extra training for themselves. Both Derek, in the Prison Service and Sue, in the police, have involved themselves in continuous training programmes to develop areas of special expertise. It seems that learning deepens commitment not only in a practical way, by bolstering self-esteem through the mastery of certain skills and the acquisition of useful knowledge, but also in a symbolic fashion, by the making of a sacrifice. The willing sacrifice of time, of mental application and, for many people, of a higher level of income while they work to achieve competence in a new field, serves as a rite of passage into another phase of their lives. And an appropriate rite of passage, in its marking of a significant life progression, helps the individual to separate his or her past from the present and the future.

This observation is given further credence by the stories of interviewees who did not particularly want to retrain but found themselves *having* to do so. Interestingly, in many instances what began as an unwelcome necessity became the key to a satisfying change of social identity.

Take Douglas: a former administrator in the Navy, he relied upon being able to use these skills as a self-employed businessman, while depending upon the complementary abilities of his wife to make a new venture work. But he found, in practice, this was not enough.

Douglas left the Navy as a Lieutenant Commander more than 10 years ago. His youthful devil-may-care attitude to life and work had changed in his early thirties when he married Celia, but, by then, he felt at a career disadvantage in competition with more consistently conscientious officers. Estimating his chances of promotion at less than 50-50, he decided to leave. Celia had worked in the world of antiques and fine art and still had contacts in the field and it was this which prompted the couple to start their own business.

They began by opening a small antiques shop; Celia concentrated on buying for the shop and also buying and selling to other dealers. Douglas managed the business as a whole and the shop itself. It worked. But the more lucrative side of the venture was the dealing, and this they expanded as opportunities arose. However, they quickly became victims of their own success, for, while their business grew, their marriage diminished. Celia found herself shouldering an increasingly heavy burden. Buying often took her away from home, and with two small children, she was not always pleased to go. When she was away, Douglas would be constantly telephoning with queries – about the stock, about the children, about the current au pair – and Celia became angry and exhausted. She admits that she actively considered divorce, since she believed she was doing the lion's share of the work for small reward, and could manage better alone: 'without the emotional hassle'. Fortunately for the family, Douglas could see the way things were going and realised that he would either have to gain more 'hands on' expertise himself or employ an expensive extra member of staff.

Thus it was that Douglas put the brake on expansion and embarked on: 'the steepest learning curve of my life'. A regular evening class in London, a correspondence course and private study, together with day-to-day practical experience occupied most of his waking hours 'for the best part of – oh, three years – although you never stop learning in this business'. By this time, however, he had turned himself from an enthusiastic amateur, with limited knowledge, into an all-round, basically competent professional. Since then he has gone on to acquire 'a thorough working knowledge of the whole of the furniture side'. His learning was driven by two imperatives: to remedy an unwise business expansion and to rescue a failing marriage. In the course of it he discovered talents he never realised he possessed and developed 'a *great* respect for Celia . . .' The business, too, rode the recession of the early 1990s and now is quietly flourishing. Did he regret leaving the Navy? Would he like to go back? 'Good Lord, no! This is totally absorbing.'

A second factor which the survey looked at was the availability of suitable role models and feedback in the workplace. This was in response to a study by Roger Middleton.[6] He interviewed men and women who had given up other occupations to become artists and found that success, not only in financial terms but also in terms of happiness and personal fulfilment, was, for most of them, reclusive. Although all the interviewees desired the change, artistic endeavour is essentially reclusive. Role models vary widely in temperament and work methods and so becoming an artist is a particularly lonely business with no easy way of knowing how best to order one's life. The subjects found that the diminution of social interaction at work which gave them personal feedback, made it difficult to rebuild a distinctive concept of themselves. Though in some cases this may have been productive artistically, it seems to have contributed to the periods of depression and inactivity which were common among the group and to a few cases of near or actual breakdown.

Knowing of Middleton's findings, it was intended to include a number of would-be artists among the former military interviewees. It was thought that finding such subjects might be difficult, but, in fact, in no time at all a longer list of potential subjects was acquired by word of mouth than could be used. This seems to indicate that a small but steady number of former servicemen become self-employed artists and craftsmen. It also suggests that artistic flair and military-taught organisation and precision can co-exist productively. Three painters, a woodcarver, a photographer, an interior designer, a landscape gardener, a potter and a musician were among the interviewees; all were achieving at least adequate financial returns, and all were reporting quite high levels of personal satisfaction. These (admittedly few) subjects seemed to be doing rather better than Middleton's interviewees.

Why? What came across very strongly was the down-to-earth pragmatism of the military leavers. They had all sought mentors who were actually making a living from their art; they were all prepared to embrace a commercial approach for much of the time; they all worked regular hours in a structured fashion;

and they were all open to allied work – for example, two of the three painters made money from teaching as well as from selling their art, while the third routinely supplemented his income by picture framing.

It does indeed seem that military experience tends to equip people to make effective use of role models and feedback. Leavers appear to concentrate hard on how a new job is done, singling out people who can show them, and not being afraid to ply them with questions. This accords with service training methods and also with the need for military personnel to define and master the essentials of new tasks very quickly as they move from posting to posting.

* * *

Traditional routes or unconventional pathways? In itself, this is an irrelevant question. Leavers who opt for the unconventional pathways usually spend a considerable time thinking it over, testing their motivation. Everyone could benefit from this approach. Service personnel are, on the whole, quick to learn and they make good use of role models, instruction and feedback. Though most are reluctant to embark upon formal courses of study or retraining, those who do generally find them stimulating and useful. Most tend to be sensible and pragmatic, but this can lead to an early, cautious acceptance of unrewarding work with narrow horizons. For, if personal satisfaction and the desire to do what one considers to be a worthwhile job is low on the list of attributes *sought* from a second career, only a few lucky people will find them by happy accident.

CHAPTER 8

Wider Horizons: Goals Beyond Employment

Do we live to work or work to live? Not all of life is work. Although only a handful of interviewees had eschewed the job market altogether, a large number had settled into steady employment which was not particularly satisfying but was financing significant leisure activities. For these subjects, leisure had become as important or more important to them than work. With this in mind, we turn our attention to the question of how effective non-work goals can be in helping military leavers to adapt to civilian life.

'Most people base their self-image and are categorised by others, primarily in terms of the work they do.' (Michael Argyle).[1] If this is true for the population at large, how much more so is it for individuals whose job has encompassed a whole way of life? Former soldiers, sailors and airmen have *belonged* to the military, have surrendered a degree of personal freedom to it and they have necessarily defined themselves in terms of their rank and their responsibilities. If, when they leave, they cannot or do not wish to find work with which they can identify, is it possible for them to build an identity around some other kind of endeavour?

* * *

Richard L. left the Army several years ago and retired. He had attained senior rank but knew he would not be promoted again. In his early forties he had inherited a modest amount of agricultural land and some property (with sitting tenants). When he decided to retire, he was approaching 50 and he and his wife Pamela felt the time was ripe to return permanently to their family roots in rural England. They bought an attractive old manor house with stabling for horses and extensive if unkempt gardens and moved in the day after Richard had completed his service.

Having assets of his own, Richard can afford to live on these plus his military gratuity and pension without needing to seek an additional source of income. (He is at pains to point out that this does not mean he is a rich man, only that, provided he is careful, he has this option.) Richard and Pamela are, of course, old enough and from the appropriate social background to remember numerous country gentlemen who lived on their lands and whose main occupation was the management of an estate. They took a lead in local affairs, entertained and were entertained by other local dignitaries and rode to hounds whenever they could. In attempting to construct a similar mode of life, albeit on a much reduced scale, Richard is following in the tradition of grander family forbears and this, in itself, he feels is an achievement and 'a privilege'.

Moving into the house, Richard and Pamela immediately began restoring and refurbishing it, doing much of the work themselves, so that now it possesses a mellow, comfortable charm, sitting at the end of a long driveway, surrounded by its gardens, stables and paddock. There will always be work to do to keep the property in good order but the main effort has now been made. Richard's time is presently spent more or less as he chooses. Tasks in the house or garden occupy a portion of most days, as does reading the 'quality' newspapers and firing off letters to their editors. Pamela does most of the work with the horses and they both ride – she every day, he not quite as frequently. They attend the village church on a Sunday and she, but not he, is involved as a volunteer, arranging flowers and dusting the pews. Richard plays golf from time to time and shoots in the season. He is physically very fit but mentally seems unchallenged. His circle of friends is largely parochial and civilian. He says he is not regularly or closely in touch with many of his former Army friends and appears (though appearances may be deceptive) to prefer a quiet life.

How has he changed since leaving the military? He says not at all, but this is surely debatable. Looking at him, listening to him, it is hard to believe that he served in the *modern* Army. That only a few years ago he was involved in delicate politico-military operations in Northern Ireland and later in NATO as the barriers between East and West were finally crumbling. He talks freely and at length about his service but his tales are of soldiering as a young man in Cyprus and the Middle East (he still has a smattering of Arabic, of which he is justly proud). And he seems to look to the colonels of his youth, who had served in the far reaches of the Empire, to find role models for the persona he now adopts. The clipped accent, the upright bearing, the small moustache, the tweed jacket and plus fours, the carved walking-stick, all create the impression that he has just returned from a hill-station in British India. He has surely become more stereotypically 'Army' since leaving than he could possibly have been as a serving officer.

Richard, without doubt, is playing a part – but the performance is conducted with gusto. It is convincing, as well it might be, since it draws from his own experience as the child of a well-to-do county family and as a young man learning his soldiering in what remained of the colonies. The props are authentic and well chosen, and the setting is right.

But what about the plot? Where is it heading? Richard has plans to join a national charitable trust and possibly to stand locally as a Conservative councillor but he has made no move to do so as yet. He says he is in no hurry to undertake major commitments and is enjoying being able to please himself. His current lifestyle undoubtedly brings him pleasure, yet one can safely say that it by no means fully engages his keen intellect or his abundant energy. He seems to live a curiously detached kind of life. Although he is proud of his Army career he has no emotional ties with the present-day military, and, asked if he would choose to rejoin, he retorts: 'Out of the question!' Goals for the future seem, at best, half-hearted.

If Richard were in reality a 'career' landowner, he would have solid practical and economic problems to overcome and tangible aims in view. Pamela, who appears more thoroughly integrated into local life, is loyal and supportive, and if she is not entirely comfortable with Richard's image, she does not say so. She smiles ruefully as she describes how he has been nicknamed 'the Galloping Major' by some of their new acquaintances. She doesn't like it, though it is meant affectionately – and she realises that not too many civilians nowadays would know the difference between a Major and a more senior ranking officer anyway.

* * *

From an outsider's perspective, one may well conclude that Richard's retirement activities only partially fill the vacuum left by his departure from the military. So what is missing? Can we pinpoint the beneficial characteristics of work which people may lose when they are unemployed or retired? By the same token, can we pinpoint the characteristics of leisure which they may gain?

Michael Argyle in his work *The Psychology of Happiness* draws on many studies to extract just these features.[2] To summarise, he notes that:

Work demands effort and expertise. Work is carried out with and/or for other people and must entail some social interaction. Work has long-term goals. Given these properties, work (though not overwork) tends to be conducive to people's well-being for a number of reasons. It brings with it responsibility, variety (a dimension beyond the domestic), social intercourse, feelings of skilfullness and an impact upon the lives of others.

Leisure need have none of these qualities (for example, watching television may have none). Leisure pursuits offer nurturance and play. Nurturance may be defined as the giving and receiving of food – sustenance for the body, the mind, the emotions and the spirit. Play, on the other hand, is self-selected activity providing an element of challenge with a variety of

possible outcomes and including a degree of spontaneous decision-making. It has been claimed that leisure is a reaction to
work. That the effort of work demands the compensation of
relaxation, that the responsibility of work creates a need for
the self-centred activities of leisure, and that the long-term
goals of work produce an appetite for fun – a break from routine and a desire for the stimulation of new experience. And yet,
in life there is much cross-over: some work is good fun, and
some fun is hard work.

'Unpacked' in this way, one can begin to see the potential
psychological drawbacks to non-employment for a healthy adult
individual. Most significantly, for anyone who is losing a clear
identity and needing to construct a new persona, the loss of the
social interaction attendant upon work could be a major blow.
For it is this interaction that provides the worker with a forum
for self-presentation and gives him feedback. Here he is
expected to look and behave in a way that will promote confidence in his ability; getting it right will produce a response of
acceptance and respect. A sense of identity may thus be built up
through the imperative of projecting a certain kind of competence at work – and be reinforced by other people's belief in it.
Outside work, opportunities for serious self-presentation are
more limited, they tend to occur with less consistency, and
they often focus upon more frivolous pursuits.

* * *

Tim is a young man who left the military in his late twenties
and, with his partner Rosie, set off to sail round the world: 'A
dream come true.' Although they felt that at some stage they
would elect to turn for home and settle down, they had no
time-frame in mind and planned to live a roving existence for as
long as they could. With some savings in the bank and a steady
income from a smart London flat, they could sustain a simple
lifestyle almost indefinitely. In the event, they were away for just
over two years and it was 'a magnificent adventure'. But was it
the kind of life they would choose to live for ever? Three years
after their return, Tim grins and says, 'Oh no!'

The voyage was indeed remarkable. They experienced danger

when their rigging was damaged in a gale, they shared the awesome beauty and lonely peace of the vast oceans under the night sky. They encountered other cultures, and forged strong bonds of common humanity with complete strangers who helped them on their journey. None of this would they have missed for the world. But inevitably, there were periods of depression too and, contrary to expectations when they left, they found that their low moods became more frequent and longer-lasting the further they got into the voyage. They had thought that the initial learning-period would be the hardest phase and that once they had adjusted to the rhythms of life at sea and the minor aggravations of functioning in such cramped conditions they would be able to adopt a relaxed, unworried approach to life. In practice, the reverse happened. The early part of the voyage was exhilarating, and their tolerance of discomfort and difficulty was high. Later, they quarrelled more and enjoyed less, and it came as a relief when Rosie discovered she was pregnant. Their spirits rose again as they made for home and parenthood.

On their return, Tim quickly found temporary work selling insurance, but since the birth of his son and his marriage to Rosie, he has begun professional training in accountancy. It is a sharp contrast to his footloose existence of a few years ago; his parents, he says, are 'ridiculously pleased, having written me off as a no-hoper'. For himself, the beaming smile which appears as he describes his present 'boring, routine' lifestyle, belies the derogatory comment.

In retrospect, Tim believes the journey 'was simply too long . . . Australia and back would have been about right'. As it was 'we sort of lost it'. Lost what? 'Lost ourselves I suppose . . .'

Tim and Rosie continue to be enthusiastic sailors and one day would like to make another long voyage, but not yet awhile. Tim's observation that they seemed to lose themselves as the journey became longer is particularly perceptive. For Tim, who had relinquished a strong military identity, was clearly finding it hard to 'reconceptualise' himself. In the beginning, the excitement of attempting a new and difficult task and the sheer wonder of the natural world viewed at close quarters carried him forward, content with just *being*. Later on, as this began to wane, both he and Rosie were increasingly thrown back on their own inner resources, and Tim, undoubtedly uncertain about who he was and what he was becoming, fell prey to bouts of melancholy. He would not have been helped by the fact that the voyage, though rich in 'nurturance and play' experiences, was lacking in the long-term goals and purposeful social inter-action which are properties of work and which help to build and reinforce identity.

The real achievement of the journey for Tim lay in its effec-tiveness as a transition experience. Although a long and sometimes painful time (at his lowest point he did fear for his sanity) he emerged with greater self-knowledge and a positive, decisive outlook on new goals of stability, employment and par-enthood.

* * *

If sailing round the world is some people's idea of heaven, so is the prospect of spending one's days pottering in gardens – and getting paid for it. This is what Bob, at the older end of the interviewees' age range, does for a living. Bob spent the greater part of his working life in the Navy, moving up through the ranks to retire as a junior officer in his forties. Divorced, with an adult daughter, he has no one to maintain but himself and has decided to opt out of 'the rat race' and become self-employed as a jobbing gardener.

Taking what may be termed as 'recreational employment' is not uncommon among older leavers with some financial secu-rity. Apparently there is a retired Army general who, on leaving, proceeded to fulfil a boyhood ambition to become a bus-driver; and again, a brigadier who has set himself up as a cobbler in a little town in Scotland. This kind of employment seems envi-able indeed.

Bob certainly finds that an outdoor life, working at his own pace, suits him. He has long been interested in plants and flow-ers and, though not an expert, has a thorough, practical knowledge of what works. His customers are an interesting mixture – from frail elderly pensioners who cannot physically manage their gardens to well-heeled middle-class families who lack the time. He often agrees to undertake non-gardening chores as well – 'especially for my old folk – like cleaning their windows or even collecting their pensions sometimes'. By and large, he says, he is treated as a friend and neighbour, not as a hired hand: 'All my regulars know I was in the Navy – comes up in conversation all the time.' Living as he does in a part of the country with a strong naval tradition, many acquaintances and friends have connections with the service, and his background is generally well understood.

Bob's attitude towards his customers and the way they treat him is, however, revealing. He is more than happy to do the work of a gardener – which is skilled but not, for him, difficult or responsible. The job is intrinsically interesting with opportunities for creativity, planning ahead, a fair degree of autonomy but also a pleasing amount of contact with clients. But proud though he is of his work, he is not prepared to be *treated* as a gardener – as if gardening is the only occupation he knows – and he refuses to work for anyone who dares to patronise him. In short, Bob does not define himself as a gardener. He is a retired naval officer, supplementing his pension by extending a former leisure skill.

Would he rejoin the Navy if he could? Bob says not, since he feels his career came to its natural conclusion and he left having accomplished all he could reasonably have expected. Even so, he admits he sorely misses the Navy as a way of life. Bob has certainly not relinquished his military persona, from which he derives a social status higher than that conferred by his current occupation. He believes that his service years were the best times of his life and cannot be surpassed, though he feels he is filling his days now, quite agreeably. And the future? 'I'm looking forward to retirement proper', he says. And why not? Only, that he is a vigorous man, with some years to go before he qualifies to draw an old-age pension.

★ ★ ★

In his mid-thirties, Ross, a former RAF NCO views non-employment from a different angle. He works hard for no pay and, in what spare time he has, he studies. Ross is a house-husband whose main occupation is the care of six-year-old Debbie and three-year-old Matthew. His wife, Kate, is a senior staff nurse who is good at her job and is prepared to work full-time, knowing that Ross is reliably at home for the family.

Ross explains how this arrangement arose at first as a temporary expedient while he was looking for work. He left the RAF with few 'civilian-friendly' qualifications and could not find employment which would pay as much as Kate could earn if she were to work full-time. Naturally enough, she was reluctant to do so, not wishing to engage, or entrust the children to full-time child care. Therefore Ross and Kate swapped roles as a temporary measure – but somewhat to their surprise, it worked unexpectedly well.

When Ross embarked upon this lifestyle, Matthew was a baby and Debbie was not yet at school. It was physically demanding, sometimes exasperating, occasionally worrying work but it was also rewarding. On the minus side, Ross found, as does many a young mother, that being with little children all day is not mentally very stimulating. Many women combat this by socialising with groups of other mothers but Ross has taken a different line. Alongside childcare he divides his working time between cultivating fruit and vegetables – which now occupy most of the garden – and studying for an Open University degree. When Matthew enters primary school Ross hopes to use his practical experience backed by an academic qualification to begin training for one of the caring professions – perhaps psychiatric nursing. It makes for a busy life: 'I used to be hopeless at fitting it all in, but now I'm quite well organised.' Whenever possible, shiftwork allowing, Kate puts the children to bed and she frequently prepares supper before 'collapsing in front of the box'. Ross, however, goes out two or three evenings a week, to meet cronies at the local pub, to attend OU tutorial groups or to play competitive squash. It is an unorthodox arrangement but one that seems to have given Ross fewer problems than the role of housewife has brought to our key interviewee, Jo Grant.

Jo is by no means alone in having found it difficult to adjust to life as a full-time housewife and mother. It is known that housewives as a group are particularly vulnerable to depression. Moreover, numerous studies have revealed that the presence of young children in a family tends to put great strain on a marital relationship.[3] How is it, then, that Ross has managed so well?

The answer may be that he has deliberately ordered and filled his time in a way that closely corresponds to work, and that Kate has helped him to do so. By working during the day but having most evenings 'off', he maintains the temporal work/leisure pattern of the market place. This also allows him to continue to associate with other working men, playing sport and going to the pub. When at home, Kate shares their domestic responsibilities and this effectively reduces the size of Ross's job, making it more manageable. But how does Kate feel?

Kate says that from a practical point of view she has no problem with their role reversal. Ross does virtually all the housework – cleaning, shopping, laundry – so that when she is around she can spend time with the children, or cook, which she enjoys, and occasionally knit or sew, which, again, she finds therapeutic: 'I sometimes resent the fact that I don't have time to go out with *my* friends. . . . and there's the children thing . . . I've got used to trusting him to look after them, but I can't help feeling jealous when he can, say, go to see them in a play at school or something at nursery and I can't . . . Ideally I'd like to reduce my hours a bit . . .'

In contrast, Jo Grant is more tightly bound by convention and by the social choices available in a military environment. Her husband Chris is often away, and when around, frequently works unsocial hours. It is therefore not possible for Jo to regularly have evenings off. Furthermore, when Chris is at home, though he helps both with chores and with childcare, he is seldom able to take more than a fleeting responsibility for either. Thus Jo has to interweave work-type and leisure-type activities in a fairly unstructured way during the course of a 24-hour day. She has lost contact with her peer group in employment, and feels that, in consequence, she has lost status and has had difficulty in maintaining her self-esteem. Voluntary work, now that her children are past babyhood, holds the prospect for Jo of achieving a more satisfying balance of activities – but, unlike Ross, she does not feel she has it yet.

* * *

Ross's situation brings to mind the experience of Malcom W. (see Chapter 4). He was invalided out of the military as a result of an accident in which he was severely burned and lost his right arm. Malcom's children are slightly older than Ross's but he, too, spends some of his time at home looking after them and doing housework. His wife, Paula, is employed for a few hours a week as a secretary, and when she is at home, Malcom works part-time as a stock controller for a local industrial enterprise. The job itself is repetitive, he says, but the social interchange in the workplace is lively and he enjoys the company of his workmates. He has, in addition, another 'hat' and it is this which gives him a real sense of identity. He is deeply involved in church work, holding the office of lay reader and helping with a multitude of activities from running the youth group to redecorating the church hall.

A no-nonsense, practical man, Malcom remembers how his accident seemed at the time 'like the end of the world'. But it made him stop and think deeply about life: 'for the first time actually'. Before that, it was Paula who had been the churchgoer, but during his long fight to regain fitness, Malcom read a good deal of 'basic theology', and what he read, he says, made sense to him. It also gave his life a dimension it had hitherto lacked – that of intellectual challenge. Since then, Malcom's church membership has become central to his life; it presents him with responsibility to carry, things to do and much to think about in getting to grips with the doctrines, teachings and traditions of Christianity.

Malcom's life is not an easy one. Money is tight, frustration and physical pain still dog him and from time to time he rages over his one-handed, fumbling ineptitude. He is certainly not a patient, saintly, serene figure but an energetic, determined battler. His battle, however, is clearly taking him forward. He sees himself primarily in terms of his religious commitment and his goals are likewise to do with the church. He senses no vocation to move towards ordination: 'Really, I'm an ordinary bloke and I make my best contribution as I am . . .', but he does see himself contributing in a lay capacity to the wider Christian community in a variety of ways, both administrative and pastoral, and the possibility of doing so gives him great satisfaction. Malcom talks about his military past with remarkable lightness and humour (most of his reminiscences, save that of the accident, are funny). There is no sign of bitterness; instead, he observes that without the events of the past he would not have achieved the richness of the present.

★ ★ ★

Malcom is one of a number of interviewees who took routine employment on leaving the armed forces but used the security it brought to give them a freedom to undertake more rewarding work on a voluntary basis.

Jason qualified as a diving instructor while he was in the military and when he left, found a job with an 'Outward Bound' type of organisation. However, the seasonal bias of the work resulted in periods of unemployment during the winter months, causing financial – and emotional – insecurity. A long-term relationship with his girlfriend broke up amid much sorrow and mutual recrimination and Jason himself came near to breaking point. Emerging from this distressing time, Jason settled for stable, if uninspiring, work as a security guard and soon afterwards met Ellie, his wife-to-be.

He was not, however, stretched by his work and was bored and restless, until a former colleague asked him if he was interested in helping with a scheme to give disabled and disadvantaged youngsters experience of water sports. Jason was inclined to refuse, since he would receive expenses only and would be expected to work alongside paid instructors who 'were no better qualified than me'. But eventually he was persuaded to help, 'just the once . . .', and that was several years ago. Since then, he has assisted on many courses and is now particularly adept at working with disabled participants. He works with as much care in a voluntary capacity as he did as a professional – and esteems it more highly than his salaried work. Although he makes no money from it, his status as a volunteer gives him a degree of flexibility and a value to the scheme as a whole that is different from that of the paid staff, and special. In fact, when Jason talks about his job as a security guard, one would deduce that he elects to do it because it keeps him alert and in trim for his main occupation – as a volunteer.

* * *

Goals beyond employment: how useful are they to the process of adjustment to civilian life? Can they take the place of work-related goals?

The case histories in this chapter demonstrate that it is perfectly possible to attain pleasure and a degree of happiness, engaging chiefly or entirely in leisure-type pursuits. But life is not only about happiness, it is also about growth; and growth, it could be argued, is the product of planning, effort and social responsibility. If people decide to avoid this, it is their own choice and it would be a gross impertinence to criticise. Nevertheless, one cannot help but suspect that in choosing to ignore their potential for growth, people who pursue only happiness, are opting for quite a limited life. Is this a prejudiced judgement?

Returning to Michael Argyle's work on the nature of happiness, it would appear that individuals who express the greatest occupational satisfaction are involved in activities which combine the beneficial characteristics of both work and leisure.

To live *contented* lives, people need to feel wanted and appreciated by others, they need to give and receive friendship, they need to direct a high proportion of their own actions and they need to refresh themselves in play. Although these are features of most people's *leisure*, some jobs incorporate these elements too, so perhaps it is not surprising that: 'The most satisfied people at work are university teachers, scientists, clergymen and other professional people like doctors and lawyers.' (Argyle)[4]

To live *purposeful* lives, individuals need to use and hone their skills, they need to make or provide things for others, and they require long-term goals. And though these are features of most people's *work*, some leisure pursuits have similar properties. It therefore comes as no surprise to learn that the most satisfying leisure activities are religion, voluntary work, making and/or repairing things, participating in performing arts or representative-level sport, and specialist clubs and classes such as chess, archaeology or conservation.[5]

Which brings us finally to the simple conclusion that, *chosen wisely*, an absorbing, purposeful occupation outside the bounds of conventional work, *can* form the basis of a new life-direction for a military leaver, and *can* help him or her to build a new sense of personal identity.

CHAPTER 9

Family Complications

We have already observed that moving out of the military world is a watershed event for the whole family. To a greater or lesser extent family members will all have been affected by the demands which the forces make upon the time, energies and loyalties of their personnel. Accustomed to living with this, the cessation of such demands will inevitably dislocate the internal dynamics of family life.

> It was weird to have Dad about the place all the time . . . When he was in the Army he used to be away a lot and it would just be Mum and us . . . That was normal . . .

These comments from Will, who was 15 at the time his father left the military. Will regards his unusual (by civilian standards) childhood as having been exceptionally happy and stable. He and his sister moved with their parents, 'following the flag' from posting to posting in the UK and overseas, adjusting every two years or so to different houses, new schools, other friends, different teachers. He never actually liked moving but did become quite adept at fitting in to new situations quickly and without fuss. Then, at the age of 11 it was boarding school and, for term-time at least, an element of continuity, underpinned by the security of family life, wherever home happened to be.

When Will's father came out of the Army he no longer received government help towards the cost of his children's boarding education and though he promised to try and maintain them at school, there was, Will recalls 'a definite sense of relief when I decided to do my sixth form at the local college'.

Educationally, the move was not as disruptive as it was feared and Will achieved good academic results which paved the way for university. Socially, however, Will says:

> It was a disaster. . . . Living at home was a nightmare . . . College was awful . . . It wasn't that – I mean there were some really good people there but – well, for a start you were looked on as a real ★★★ if you were interested in any of the college activities. Sport or plays. And if you weren't into drugs.

Not being part of the 'in' group at college upset Will and must have shaken his confidence somewhat. It probably wouldn't have mattered if home had been the steady, reliable place he had always known, but it wasn't. His father experienced considerable difficulty in finding suitable employment and was periodically in and out of work. Each setback brought tirades of rage against the government, the EC, students, racial minorities, the media – and of course, those nearest to hand, his own family. Home became a place 'fraught with aggro', and Will was relieved to get away to university.

Returning for his first Christmas, Will found his parents on the brink of separation and, when the vacation was over, he could not concentrate on his studies. Some stalwart undergraduate friends and an understanding tutor helped to keep him going, but the ensuing months were punctuated with missed work deadlines and poor marks so that eventually he was required to repeat the year.

And his parents? Later that same year, a windfall helped. Will's elderly grandmother died and with the proceeds of the sale of her house, his mother bought a flat in London. She spent time there but did not separate from his father and gradually the flat became, and remains, a base for Will, his sister and their mother. Will's father, on the pretext of disliking the city, never goes, and Will seldom visits his parents' home.

Today, Will has graduated and is working, his sister is engaged to be married, his parents are still together and he has a good deal of contact with his mother and sister. In practical terms, a reconstitution of the affinities of his childhood. Emotionally, though, Will's relationship with his father is completely different. As a child, he adored him, even though his frequent absences made him a remote figure in comparison to his mother. Now, however, Will does not hold him in high regard and the remoteness of the relationship is a matter of choice – certainly on Will's part. His sister has maintained a more affectionate bond with her father but even she sees little of him. The family no longer functions as a unit – but it still exists. It could have been worse.

* * *

That 'changing step' is a stressful business for leavers and their families is undeniable. Nobody knows how many military marriages break up when families move away from the service environment. SSAFA (the Soldiers', Sailors' & Airmen's Families Association) officials believe that the number is quite large and this worries them. They are currently co-ordinating research into the whole area of military marriages in order to target help better – but it is a long-term programme and the armed forces themselves are quite naturally more anxious to support initiatives which focus upon the needs of serving rather than of former military personnel.

Certainly, during the course of this study, numerous examples were found (without any need to actively seek them out) of couples who had split up in the aftermath of discharge from the military. This does not, in itself, *prove* anything but it does seem to indicate that marital breakdown during the process of adjustment to civilian status is by no means an uncommon occurrence.

If this is so, perhaps it is possible to isolate the peculiar strains inherent in the process, which put such intolerable pressure on some marriages. Does it appear, for instance, that many failed or troubled relationships were actually vulnerable for one reason or another, long before the couple moved away from the military?

This seems a possible scenario but one which is difficult to investigate. Marriage by its very nature involves the continual resolution of actual or potential conflict between partners. Every couple have their own notion of what is, for them, 'productive tension' and at what point this turns into an unhappy and unacceptable level of strife. There are no clear yardsticks for measuring marital discord. It is only by eliciting individuals' own perceptions of change in a marriage that we can proceed at all. Thus if someone *says* that his marriage, whatever its problems, was not threatened with breakdown while he was in a military environment and that it was the alteration of the context of the marriage – from military to civilian – which he could not cope with, then one must take this as being broadly true. The consequence of making this assumption is that, even allowing for the fact that people look for concrete reasons to explain failures, and that leaving the military is a major life event on which all manner of difficulties may be blamed, it is still the case that for many interviewees, leaving had had a hugely destabilising effect on a formerly stable marriage.

* * *

It is conventional wisdom that the military leaver needs the support of his or her family to assist in the process of adjustment to civilian life. The reality seems to be that, very often, spouses or partners are in no state to give it, being preoccupied with the affects of change in their own lives. And this is evident no matter what the *apparent* disruption to the partner's own lifestyle. It seems that serious marital conflict is as common in instances where a partner is 'anchored' (i.e., continues to live in the same place, pursue the same occupation and socialise with the same friends) but has to integrate this established way of life into a new whole as the leaver constructs a place in it, as it is in instances where couples are adjusting 'in parallel' or adjusting 'together'. By 'adjustment in parallel' is meant the situation whereby the family moves to a new location on leaving, and both husband and wife (and children too) set about forging a settled civilian occupation and lifestyle independently from one another, though at the same time. 'Adjustment together' refers to those couples who, on leaving, form a working partnership – for example, running a pub – alongside their longer-standing marriage. None of these situations is easy; each has its advantages, each its pitfalls.

★ ★ ★

The following three case studies relate experiences which were more painful than those of the majority of respondents. However, aspects of their stories recurred frequently, in milder form, in the recollections of others. On this topic, some of the most enlightening conversations were with the now-adult children of military marriages who could clearly remember this period of their family lives and were perhaps slightly less inhibited than their parents in describing what happened and how it felt.

Ginny is in her mid-twenties. Her father left the military six years ago as a senior NCO who had progressed as far as he was able in his field. He was required to leave but was given ample time to make plans. A calm and methodical man who had worked all his life in an administrative capacity, he was offered more than one civilian post, in advance of his discharge date. He accepted a job as an administrative assistant with a City of London institution and the family moved from a married quarter estate to a house in the suburbs.

Ginny's father found much in his job that was reminiscent of service life. His boss – a former Army officer – was easy to get on with, the work drew upon his proven organisational capabilities and he enjoyed the occasional social and ceremonial events in which he played a part. Ginny at this time was already living away from home, training to be a teacher. Soon after the move to London, her younger brother also went away to study. This left Barbara, Ginny's mother, at home.

Ginny describes how her mother was the daughter of Army parents and had spent her whole life in a military environment. Although widely travelled, bright and energetic, her only experience of work – paid or voluntary – was under the auspices of the military. Latterly, as the wife of a senior NCO working in a key position on camp, she had accepted opportunities to help in the organisation of community events and had achieved a high profile in her own right within that community. Now, in her forties, she faced multiple losses as her children left home, her husband pursued a career which did not involve her, and the familiar, tightly knit world of the Army camp and the married patch with its self-absorbed busyness, its tittle-tattle and its warmth was replaced by the strangeness of life in suburbia.

Barbara did make an effort. For example, she joined the staff of a charity shop for a few hours a week as a volunteer, and enrolled in a keep-fit class, but none of the activities she tried could begin to replace what she had lost. Despite being reasonably occupied, outside the military she had no 'reflected' status, and as a newcomer in a permanent community (as opposed to a continually changing Army camp) she had not yet earned more than a peripheral role in the groups she had joined. Used to moving house and being 'in the thick of things' in next to no time, she felt her new neighbours were unfriendly and she was perplexed and miserable.

Remembering how, on weekends at home from college, Ginny noticed her mother becoming 'fussily houseproud', she says: 'I put it down to the fact that, for the first time, she had a house she could *keep* . . .'

But gradually she realised there was something wrong. Barbara was cleaning and tidying obsessively and, when not doing that, was spending long periods of time sitting at her kitchen table, staring out of the window. Ginny was reluctant to say or do anything: 'I was afraid . . .', and when she did confront her mother and ask what was wrong she found herself 'unlocking the floodgates'. Barbara could not explain anything but simply wept and wept.

Ginny's father admitted that her mother had 'not been herself', but he hadn't known why, and hadn't broached the subject with her. Maybe he too was afraid. Barbara continued to cry, clean the house and gaze out of the window but when she spoke, she made little sense. Eventually, against Barbara's wishes, a doctor was called and together they persuaded her to accept a short admission to a psychiatric unit.

The whole episode was a tremendous shock to the family on several counts. First, the change in Barbara over the course of a year or so had been dramatic. From being the cheerful, resourceful linchpin of a family and its wider community, she had become a lonely, frightened obsessive. Secondly, the family had watched it happen. They felt 'horribly guilty' and, in a way, believed they were being punished. It didn't seem fair, for they, too, were leading changed lives and had problems of their own to resolve. But now they had to devote time and attention to Barbara – Barbara on whom they were accustomed to rely as a pillar of strength.

Furthermore, there is, in Ginny's narration, an ambivalence, even now, about the nature of her mother's illness. She clearly wonders how much control Barbara had over the timing and severity of her breakdown. That she was ill was certain, but to what extent was her eventual behaviour a desperate, attention-seeking gesture? And does it matter? To Ginny, it does, for her mother's breakdown brought her to regard her parents in a different light and left her with a lingering sense of insecurity. It precipitated an uncomfortably rapid entry into adulthood with the realisation that she could no longer be emotionally dependent upon her parents.

Barbara's recovery was rapid – up to a point. Her illness seems to have been a comparatively straightforward reaction to obvious stress. A combination of drug therapy and TLC (tender, loving care) enabled her to regain functional fitness quite quickly and she has not had any severe recurrence requiring admission to hospital. However, Ginny feels that even though this happened several years ago, her mother has still not found new direction and purpose in her life. She worries when she telephones and finds her listless and 'flat': 'I don't think there's anything I can do. I wish Dad would do more . . . I feel so – inadequate. . . .'

★ ★ ★

Ginny's story vividly illustrates one of the main risks associated with 'parallel adjustment' – that different family members adjust at different speeds under different circumstances and that it is all too easy for one of them to be left behind. Sometimes the rest of the family may genuinely not notice, sometimes they may react with denial and *choose* not to notice; sometimes they may try to help. Quite frequently, however, the help they do give is limited because much of their energy is necessarily directed towards the resolution of their own uncertainties.

Is it therefore not far easier for people to embark upon the process of adjustment together? A joint venture, a new start, a team effort. Some of the most 'successful' adapters in the study took this route – Angus, the vet, Peter, the woodcarver and their wives for example – and it does have several advantages.

When a couple undertake a project together, they relinquish a measure of security in terms of the other's independent earnings, so their commitment to the work they have chosen has to be wholehearted. Owing to the greater risk of having all their eggs in one basket, their enterprise is likely to have been reasonably well thought out beforehand – which in itself, increases their chances of success. Then, *needing* one another in practical ways, depending on the other person to pull his or her weight, demands a fair degree of communication. Talking about day-to-day problems does also open the door to the voicing of fears, hopes and expectations – which helps to prevent them from being bottled up and becoming one individual's 'hidden agenda'. And, finally, working together, knowing the same people and negotiating a similar learning curve promotes a converging outlook on life and shared definitions of success. So far, so good, but this last factor, which can be so positive, seems also to be the greatest drawback to changing step together.

Sharing the same outlook and agreeing on what constitutes success is all very well – until, in spite of the best efforts of all concerned, it fails to materialise, and a shared perspective on failure may make the whole venture vulnerable to collapse in a bad patch. Since, when difficulties arise, objective assessment is needed to tackle them – and that is just what two people in the same boat tend to lack.

It is what happened to Tim and Rosie (see Chapter 5) who were *literally* in the same boat. Feeling that their adventure which started so well, was not achieving anything, what they needed was another perspective on their situation. Until it came in the shape of prospective parenthood, they were unable to escape from a downward spiral of despondency and, far from being able to give mutual support, each inadvertently reinforced the other's sense of failure, *because* they had become so close.

Jamie and Beth's experience echoes this too. In the RAF, Jamie was a cook and Beth a steward. From the moment they started going out together they talked about running a hotel or a restaurant. When they left (taking an opportunity to go before their contracts expired – with the RAF reducing staff and putting much of its mess catering into the hands of private-sector operators) they married, pooled what capital they had, and took out a substantial mortgage on a guest house in a south coast resort town.

Their first year of business was remarkably good, though there was predictably little activity during the winter months. To tide them over, Jamie took bar work and Beth – expecting a baby – managed the occasional guests single-handedly. The second summer was wet and, for lack of passing trade, income was down on their first season – a worrying phenomenon not helped by a gloomy bank manager who began to undermine their confidence, not by anything he *did*, but by his constant, pessimistic warnings.

Then, the following winter, a minor disaster. The house, a pretty, early-Victorian building a few streets behind the seafront, suffered storm-damage against which they were inadequately insured. Roof repairs cost more than they could afford and they were closed for far too long. By the time they reopened, two other houses in the same area had entered the bed and breakfast market and trade inevitably suffered. Jamie kept his bar job into the summer to help maintain a cash-flow, but this made life difficult for Beth, who was bearing most of the burden of running the business and coping with a lively toddler. The season left them both exhausted and, at the end of it, they still had formidable debts to repay and nothing to spend.

Beth remembers how , one evening, when Jamie came home, they decided their business had failed. They were not enjoying life, working long hours and being always worried about money; they could make a better living working for someone else. So they sold up. Jamie took a job as a chef in the kitchens of a prestigious hotel while Beth found part-time employment in the tourist information office. They moved into a rented bungalow, cleared their debts and for the first time in their married life had a holiday. It was a huge relief.

Now, however, Beth wishes they had not given up quite so readily. As employees, she and Jamie may have fewer financial problems but they also have little freedom and no prospects. She recalls that the success of their first season demonstrated their ability to make a business work, and that much of the ill-fortune which befell them subsequently was outside their control. In retrospect she believes they should not have allowed each other (plus the gloomy bank manager) to acquiesce in a general verdict of failure which resulted in their 'baling out' when they were not actually heading for anything as catastrophic as a crash.

Instead, she thinks that they should have been bolder, should have asked for a bigger loan for the damaged house, to extend it and reopen as a small hotel. This would have put them above the competition which sprang up when they were closed and would also have allowed them to accommodate 'overspill' conference guests from the larger hotels whose year-round trade now rests heavily on the conference market. Would it have worked? Who knows?

Beth would very much like to start again, despite the hard work and the burden of renewed financial pressures. She and Jamie are older, wiser, and, she thinks, more resilient. Jamie, however, will have none of it. He is content to be a chef, in regular employment and regards their last year in the guest house as having been a nightmare. He is in no hurry to recall it, let alone risk a repetition. Beth finds herself getting angry at her husband's steadfast refusal to even discuss the matter and she is deeply disappointed in his willingness to abandon their dreams for good. Stalemate.

* * *

A substantial number of servicemen have, by the time they leave, settled their families ahead of them. Many naval families (like Frank Warrell's) never moved anyway, and so it is a fairly common situation for a partner to have been living and working in a civilian setting for a considerable period before being joined by the leaver. For the leaver, moving into civilian life alongside an 'anchored' family can have many pluses.

A civilianised spouse can provide valuable practical aid. Frank Warrell's wife, having lived in their home-locality throughout her life, had many helpful friends with contacts prepared to give information, advice and even actual job opportunities. Socially, an 'anchored' spouse with a circle of friends and acquaintances to whom the leaver can be introduced, can provide a ready-made civilian 'frame of reference' with approaches to life and work that differ from one another and from the military norm.

But if, from a practical point of view the 'anchored' family seems to offer the leaver the smoothest start to the next phase of his or her life, from an emotional angle, it may not.

Although few couples embark on a marriage with the idea of conducting a semidetached relationship, this is, in fact, what many military couples learn to live with. For naval families in particular, the service takes its members away from home repeatedly and for long periods – and the cycle of separation and reunion is often not only *endured*, but in lots of ways, it comes to be *enjoyed*. Indeed, for wives of members of all three services, it is often less strange to be running a household with a husband coming and going, than it is to be finally together 'for good'. Then, for both parties, late in the relationship, the business of merging semidetached lives into a coherent whole, begins in earnest – and it may be hard.

An interview with Viv, a sensible, practical woman in her

fifties reveals how an ordinary and, hitherto stable, family was 'knocked sideways' by the difficulties of integrating two military leavers.

Viv's husband Jock, retired from the military as a middle–ranking officer several years ago, having served until he was 49. For most of their married life Viv had followed the flag with her husband. The greater part of their two daughters' childhood years was spent in Germany. Jock's last tours of duty, however, were back in the UK and the family moved into a cottage in Buckinghamshire. Viv, a nurse, found employment at a local hospital, the girls left home for university and Jock came and went – as he always had.

With the end of his military career in sight, Jock was delighted when he was offered a sales job in the defence industries. He happily took early retirement and became a civilian.

'In actual fact . . .', Viv says, 'our lives didn't change at all . . .' He went away on technical trials, he visited the MoD, he mixed with many of the same people: 'It was perfect.'

But *Options for Change*, in the wake of the collapse of the Soviet threat, hit civilian as well as military jobs. Drawdown brought redundancies and Jock was among the first to go. It was a blow. However, he was financially well-compensated and there was no pressure on him to find another job; he decided to take his time and look for something congenial.

Meanwhile, Viv and Jock's younger daughter Abigail graduated from university, landed an enviable job in the media and moved into an up-market flat in north-west London. They were pleased and proud of their high-flying, career-minded daughter – pleased, but not altogether surprised as she had always been a single-minded, ambitious youngster. They *were* surprised, when shortly afterwards she became engaged and married to Toby, a fellow student at university who had joined the Army on a short-service commission. Of course they gave their blessing, but they were slightly uneasy.

Toby's Army service took him away from Abigail in London quite frequently but she was prepared for that. She stayed put in her flat, worked at her career and enjoyed the periods of time they spent together.

She was also a great emotional support to her mother, as Viv struggled to cope with Jock's being at home – all day, every day: 'He completely took over the house. I'd go out to work in the morning and come back to find he'd reorganised the kitchen or replanted the flower-beds . . . .' She introduced him to her friends: 'but he didn't like any of them'.

Instead, he became a 'regular' at a pub not far away which was frequented by servicemen: 'He used to come home with all the gossip . . . I was bored to tears with it . . .'

In the end, without his having done anything to instigate it, Jock was head-hunted for a second time. A small aviation company (staffed almost entirely by former servicemen) wanted his expertise, and though the salary was 'on the low side', the job was flexible and interesting, with a certain amount of travelling away from home. He hesitated but was eventually persuaded to accept: 'And thank God he did . . .', Viv says, 'I was at the end of my tether.'

Viv and Jock are now living once more according to their old, customary pattern, but that is by no means the end of the story. As Jock re-entered a familiar world, his son-in law, Toby, left it. Toby had never intended making a full career in the Army and in common with others of his type, he had contacts in the City. On leaving the military to take a job in banking, he expected, Viv explains: 'to settle down with Abigail in Surrey, raise a family and play golf . . .'

Abigail, it seems, was appalled. She had absolutely no intention of forsaking her career, her flat or her friends and she had no desire whatsoever at her stage of life to produce children. Endless, pointless quarrels ensued. Viv has her own views on the matter. She thinks that her fiercely independent daughter should never have married the thoroughly decent but intensely conventional Toby in the first place. Viv believes she was looking for an element of security at that time (her father had just been made redundant) and to some extent blames herself and Jock for not having been able to provide it.

Nevertheless, according to Viv, Abigail had relished being married to a soldier. She had been more than willing to attend regimental cocktail parties, dinners and balls, had skilfully sidestepped pressures to accompany her husband by pleading special consideration for the demands of her journalistic work. She had taken the separations from Toby calmly and had revelled in their subsequent, romantic reunions.

In the long run, Abigail was probably not the right partner for Toby – in or out of the Army – but the break-up of their marriage, when it came, caused a lot of unhappy soul-searching. Toby met and had an affair with another woman whom he then wanted to marry. He presented Abigail with the facts of the situation, and he wished also to explain his point of view to his in-laws. He visited their house, but it was painful, since Abigail too was temporarily in residence, having come home, hurt and humiliated, to nurse her wounds: 'We all sat round a table in the garden – Toby and Abigail, Jock and me – it was this beautiful sunny day . . .'

They managed to talk things through; there was a tearful, dignified leave-taking, and the young people's marriage was, in effect, over. Viv could see both sides of the story only too clearly:

> I know my daughter – marrying him was a mistake – but it might have had a chance if things had – just gone on for a while . . . With Toby coming out [of the military] – well, I *know* how impossible it is . . . Hell-on-wheels . . . I'd just gone through all that myself . . . I couldn't *believe* it was happening to us again . . .

But it isn't over yet. Although Viv's husband Jock has no immediate plans to retire, he can't go on for ever – and then he and Viv will be back to being together all the time. And a final twist: Abigail's elder sister has just started going out with a young RAF officer, the son of another military family whom they have known since their days in Germany.

* * *

It would be hard to determine exactly how common it is for military leavers to experience *serious* family difficulties. This survey came across numerous stories of disharmony, though the majority of problems were not as intractable as the ones described in this chapter. But clearly they were not isolated cases, neither did they happen only to families made vulnerable by pre-existing tensions.

All families are different. And the way in which any particular one has coped with the demands of a military environment must surely determine its own, unique (and one hopes temporary) imbalance when the all-pervading influence of the military is withdrawn.

There can thus be no standard prescriptions for avoiding difficulties. In fact, it is pretty safe to say that most families *will* experience problems of some kind on leaving. So are there any prescriptions for at least mitigating them? Yes, the evidence of families such as the Moorcrofts and others, who managed to remain steady when the going was hard, shows that there are sensible, unremarkable, loving and caring things which families can do to protect and sustain one another. And in a crisis nearly all families do them – but forget the rest of the time. Leaving the military is a kind of bereavement, and in common with reactions to a death in the family, people tend to rally round immediately. But for the bereaved, the toughest time is often not the immediate aftermath of a loss but its long-term effects – one, two, three or more years down the line.

Families, when they look out for one another, are the best providers of help and support in times of trouble. But the truth is that families in adversity may expend so much energy in managing their individual daily lives that they become simply too tired to talk *together* when they have the opportunity. As a result, problems can develop almost unnoticed, simmering away until they erupt with destructive effect. Thus *talking* – regularly and routinely – about the humdrum minutiae of 'changing step' can keep each member of the family in touch with the moods of the others. Support for one frustrated or unhappy person cannot be forthcoming if no one is aware of the need for it.

Ginny's story illustrates, too, how easy it is for families to ignore another's distress through fear of the possible size of the problem and doubt as to how it may be solved. But ignoring someone's unhappiness only increases his or her feelings of isolation and makes the situation many times worse. It takes confidence, but the gentle employment of a listening ear; the giving of time, consideration and kindness can, of themselves, pull another family member through. The reassurance that troubled people do not face the world alone is often all that is needed to give them the strength to tackle their difficulties themselves.

And if there *is* a concrete problem which is beyond the capacity of the family to solve? In that case, two or more heads are better than one when it comes to finding the person or the organisation that can help.

Awareness, patience, kindness and, if necessary, the mobilising of practical help. It sounds so simple; exactly what families are *for*. In reality, families so frequently fail one another. People worry in case by acknowledging a spouse's or child's uncharacteristic behaviour they may seem to be condoning it; they become exasperated; they focus on the problem and not the person: in short, they get out of the habit of really communicating with one another. No family is immune to these insensitivities, but forewarned is forearmed. Leaving the world of the military will have repercussions for every member of the family, no matter how they felt about their military link or the prospect of its severance.

Families who survive the peculiar pressures of service life tend to be extraordinarily close and strong. But paradoxically, it is in some instances those very pressures that have helped to make them so. Take them away and family solidarity may threaten to crumble. A sobering thought.

A caring family is the best back-up that any leaver can have. But it must not be forgotten that all the members of the family are leavers too, and all of them both need, and can give, support.

CHAPTER 10

The 'Gift of Continued Life': Conclusions

> Against the astonishment of this unasked-for continued life we did not know how to turn our gift to account . . .
>
> (T.E. Lawrence)

Having quoted Lawrence of Arabia in the opening chapter of this book, it is to him we turn again at its end.[1] For he both observes and shares the debilitating emotional emptiness of the dedicated soldier when the battle is done, and his words echo with startling clarity over the generations.

This study has taken an in-depth look into the experiences of a cross-section of military leavers. It is hoped that the results will prove interesting and useful in their detail, but no study can accomplish everything. Having depth, it lacks breadth. A relatively small number of subjects took part and the temptation to draw sweeping conclusions from the evidence of fewer than 100 interviewees in total, must be resisted.

Nevertheless, some findings do stand out. Prominent among these is the finding that, despite the availability of advice, counselling and practical resettlement courses, it is quite normal for people to leave military service without any clear view of the road ahead.

The military ethos itself discourages thoughts about civilian life. A member of the armed forces is made to feel he or she belongs to an élite, an élite which takes a pride in standing slightly apart from the society which it serves. That he (or she) has to be prepared to take life or to be killed in the course of duty, cannot allow for any wavering of commitment. An individual who harbours any doubt about the validity of what he or she is doing cannot continue for long. The military is a black-and-white world which brooks no indecision and demands complete (though not unthinking) loyalty.

The military is also a world of action, not introspection. Hi-tech equipment, modern man-management techniques and the continual review of strategic and tactical theory demand an increasing amount of academic study from servicemen and women, but everything studied has a practical application. Not for them the luxury of idle speculation or unfettered lateral thinking; for the bread-and-butter of everyday soldiering on which all else depends is standardisation: the orderly performance of practised tasks, beginning in the thoughtful atmosphere of the classroom and continuing in the relative safety of limited exercises, to bear fruit in the uncertain and potentially unnerving conditions of peacekeeping operations, or the chaos of full-scale battle. Skill and knowledge in a military setting must have utility – contemplation for its own sake is not professionally encouraged.

Certainty and action – two key features of military life. How difficult it is for those who have *chosen* this life to stand back from it long enough to begin to imagine alternatives for themselves. No wonder it seems that only a small minority of leavers are able to change step with confidence, sure of the direction their futures will take. For the many, Lawrence's words appear to describe their situation exactly. They have known that one day their service would end, they have immersed themselves in their military tasks as that end came closer, they have completed their final duties, and, on completion, have been 'given' the rest of their lives – to do with as they choose. And the term 'astonishment' does seem to sum up many people's immediate reaction quite uncannily well.

After astonishment, a host of mixed emotions: excitement,

relief, sorrow, fear. And then, comes action. Even if the leaver has not the remotest idea of what he (or she) wishes to do with this 'gift', he will want and need to *act*. And so he will instigate a chain of action and response that will carry him along – often in the first feasible direction that presents itself. Whether this is a direction that will ultimately bring a renewed sense of purpose is usually considered irrelevant at this point. There is an imperative to move; not to be *doing* can bring a terrible sense of lack of control. And for some leavers, this is as far as they get. Many do not stop – ever – to ask themselves what they could do, should do, want to do, with this astonishing gift of continued life.

Lucky ones may stumble into an occupation – paid or unpaid – which does bring fulfilment, but others may not. And, in this event, they will be reluctant or unable to let their military identities slip. Like the prisoners and the severely disabled who cling to a former sense of self, they too will retain their previous self-image, and will for ever be 'ex- service'.

But is it not a comfortable thing to be 'ex-service'? A reassuring and perfectly rational way of viewing oneself? Ask many a hard-pressed serviceman in these days of small forces, rapid reaction and fast turn-around what they dream of, and the reply is not likely to be a second career. It is far more likely to be time to spare and a settled home to possess and enjoy. A second career, however, is a necessity for most leavers. And if many of them would rather still be in the military, or else, retired, isn't it downright condescending to suggest that they should not hold tight to their 'ex-serviceness' for the rest their lives? Haven't they earned the right to maintain this persona if they wish?

Well, of course they have. But maybe there *is* another moral issue to be considered here: that of waste. For 'the gift of continued life' is not everyone's. Although the number of fatalities occurring in the course of military duty is not of alarming proportions, it would be true to say that virtually all serving personnel have known people who have lost their lives on duty. A death may form the subject of a brief, solemn news item but it is – has to be – an accepted and acceptable happening:

A Harrier jump jet on a research flight ditched in the Irish Sea off the coast of Scotland yesterday . . .

The crew of the fishing boat *Crusader* reported finding debris . . .

Witnesses said they believed the pilot averted a disaster when he came low over a caravan site, but held a steady line and with the engines still running, ditched the aircraft into the sea . . .

Fisherman Andrew Lockhead said: 'He never stood a chance.' Last night an RAF Nimrod and five lifeboats were hunting for his body . . .

(Extracts from *The Independent, The Times, Daily Telegraph* and *Daily Star*, 2 June 1995)

Servicemen are not inclined to take their survival for granted, but if and when they become leavers, perhaps they do bear a kind of moral responsibility to live their lives with all the vigour and determination that their former colleagues – casualties of war and of keeping the peace – can no longer exhibit. To do so, honours their memory.

High-flown sentiments, articulated because this study suggests that quite a worrying number of former service personnel tend not to hope or expect to derive high levels of satisfaction from their occupations and activities as civilians. Such resignation demonstrates the alienation which many of them feel (and continue to feel for years, sometimes for the rest of their lives) from the mainstream of our society.

All very well, but after the stimulating, even dangerous intensity of life in a military environment, how can civvy street not appear mundane? How did the study's 'successful adapters' find an excitement and a challenge to compare with what they had left behind? The answer is that they didn't – to begin with. New possibilities always took time to develop and new challenges could not inspire them until a fairly sure sense of direction and purpose had begun to emerge. And this required an open mind, a steady nerve, and above all, a refusal to settle for second best.

★ ★ ★

There seems to be a general expectation on the part of leavers that 'changing step' will happen naturally. Perhaps they recall joining the forces and remember how quickly they came to think, feel and act like a soldier, sailor or airman. Perhaps they forget – or never realised – that this was largely due to the intensive training which they received. Perhaps they forget how this training was renewed and reinforced at regular intervals throughout their service. Such conditioning having been an integral part of their lives, it is naive for leavers to assume that its effects will just simply and naturally fall away as they swap their uniforms for civilian clothes – but this is precisely what many do assume.

Deconditioning is a process that will not just proceed of its own accord. It has to be desired; it has to be worked at. It is a process that is more gradual but probably more difficult than *becoming* a serviceman – gentler in that it can be taken at the individual's own pace; harder, in that each leaver has to decondition himself; no one will do it to him or for him.

The study also confirms that, in line with previous research on adaptation to major life changes, three distinct aspects to the task are discernible: confrontation, disengagement and resocialisation. Moreover, while overlapping a good deal, they arise more or less in that order. And there are no short cuts; in particular, no way of proceeding from confrontation to resocialisation without travelling the uncomfortable path of transition through disengagement. It seems that a few leavers choose at the outset not to begin this journey – and a significant proportion opt, along the way, not to see it through.

* * *

At the time of going to press, Dave Lock is missing. That is to say, his probation officer does not know his precise whereabouts. As he is still subject to a probation order, he will, in due course, be found by the police – but the search is hardly a priority for them – or, sadly, for anyone else.

Dave disappeared from the hostel for the homeless which was temporarily giving him shelter a few weeks ago. According to the staff there, he had met a young woman on the streets who said she had relatives in America and he had talked about going with her to start a new life. Since the pair of them have only their income support on which to subsist, America is not a likely destination. His new friend, however, is said to come from the Gloucester area, and it is the Gloucestershire police in particular who are keeping a lookout for them.

That Dave is not alone, that he has found the motivation and energy to make a move, that he has recently expressed a desire for a new start, is all to the good. It is not beyond the bounds of possibility that *this* time, with *this* friend, he may begin the slow climb back towards a more sober, stable, caring and cared-for existence. But his probation officer is not holding his breath . . .

* * *

Confrontation

Dave was one interviewee who had not had a 'satisfactory' military career, neither was his leave-taking an expected or well-planned event. He did not subsequently manage to find his feet in civilian life either. But among the respondents were a significant number who had come to terms with disillusionment or disappointment in the military and had been able to forge a satisfying lifestyle for themselves afterwards. Nick P.[2] for example, Sandra J.[3] Malcom W.[4] and John T.[5] who is now pursuing a career in the arts.

It seems that some people are able to find the inner strength to use misfortune as a spur, and in the case of the people mentioned, they had painfully but purposefully faced the shortcomings of their military experience and had determined to draw a line under them. They had gone on to disengage and resocialise because they were driven by a sense of injustice or failure and hungered after compensatory achievement. 'Successful' leavers, lacking that impulsion, required different reasons to bring them to the point of confrontation with the inevitability of change.

A strong and growing desire to fulfil a different ambition, outside the forces, has proved an equally effective motive for confronting the end of a military career – witness Peter the woodcarver,[6] Geoff the clergyman[7] or Angus Moorcroft the vet.

But most leavers lack such clarity of intent. The desire to move on from a military life seems, more usually, to arise gradually, after discharge, as civilian opportunities appear. Then, slowly, subjects may begin to conceive of themselves as players on a different stage. Thus for many leavers, confrontation – the realisation that a military career is ending – occurs not before but after their last day of service. The study suggests, however, that the formal marking of a leaver's departure may do much to assist the business of confrontation and ease the process of disengagement.

★ ★ ★

Rite of Passage

Endings and beginnings. Neither Dave Lock nor Jo Grant was given a formal farewell at the end of their military service. Angus Moorcroft had a low-key lunch party and Frank Warrell was dined out on board ship. It is worth restating the fact that every interviewee whose leaving had been formally marked, expressed appreciation of this. In fact, it seems that such an occasion frequently attains a growing symbolic importance over the years.

A few subjects who had been disappointed at the lack of a significant farewell had invested other, related events with the symbolism of a rite of passage. A notable example is Bill, who bought his own beer on leaving (see Chapter 4) and not surprisingly, felt slightly dissatisfied with the occasion. Some time later, when he joined a defence-related firm, he accompanied his new boss on a visit to the MoD in London, for talks and a business lunch. In familiar surroundings but playing a different role, Bill felt the day was 'a kind of hand-over' and in retrospect, it was that occasion which, marked, for him, his passage into civilian life.

Another subject who had had no formal farewell, suddenly, several years after leaving, decided to drive his wife and children a hundred miles or so to RAF Swinderby, to show them the place where he joined up. They stopped near the main gate for a while, had lunch at a nearby pub and then went home. He reminisced a lot that day and says that he was astonished at how intensely important it was to him, both at the time and since.

Thus although an official leave-taking is extremely helpful, if it disappoints or fails to happen, it does seem possible to create an equally significant alternative experience (such as the 'hand-over' or the 'pilgrimage' described above). In fact, the return to Swinderby suggests that something of this nature is well worth doing, even if a considerable time has elapsed since discharge.

★ ★ ★

Disengagement

Given that servicemen and women normally exhibit a high level of attachment to the military and are usually institutionalised, it follows that disengagement is likely to be a very uncomfortable period for most leavers. It is, of necessity, a rootless time, and for those used to security this is disquieting at best, at worst terrifying. Small wonder that, beset by doubts and fears, many leavers conclude that their lives are going wrong and deliberately reduce their openness to change, just as they approach a point where they *could* change.

It is easy to state that disengagement is a transitory period, to be welcomed and used – but harder by far for an individual to believe this, when he or she is living through it. The inevitable emotional vacillation between an attachment to what *has been* and a commitment to what *could be* is wearing. It is also worrying for mature people who, feeling they ought to be more sure of themselves, tend to regard their vulnerability as shameful.

All leavers possess some time between their realisation that military service is ending and their achievement of a settled way of life as a civilian. Most people have a good deal of time between these two events – more time than is comfortable, and so it is rushed, it is denied, it is cut short. It is a rare individual who instinctively appreciates the benefits of a period as a 'displaced person', and who will seek at this time to retreat from the rat race for a while to order his or her thoughts.

Comfortingly, however, it seems there is no time-limit on disengagement. It may profitably begin as soon as a leaver has confronted the reality of the end of his or her military career, but this pace is not essential. Indeed, there can be no progress until the leaver is ready, and this may not be for months or even years after discharge.

And when a leaver is ready, then what? It is a paradox that the people who have managed most effectively to 'change step' have actually spent a lot of time (by design or accident) during 'disengagement' going over the events, the motives, the high and the low points of their military service and their lives in general. Consciously looking backwards, putting things into perspective, trying to make sense of it all. Exactly what the 'common sense brigade' would deem to be unhealthily intro-spective and a pointless squandering of time which could be spent in 'getting on with life'. But here, the common sense brigade is, categorically, wrong.

Angus Moorcroft, Frank Warrell and other successful adapters who appear in this study, all took time to mull over their life experiences. Both Angus and Frank did so while still serving; they were alike in coming to recognise what it was they had wanted from the military on joining. They also shared the satisfaction of having achieved their initial aims and a realisa-tion that, for them, the time was ripe to move on.

Peter Marris, emphasises the importance of looking back-wards at major turning points in life. He dismisses well-meaning attempts to discourage this impulse and main-tains that, far from being self-indulgent or irrational it is 'as necessary for survival as adaptability'. This is because: 'We assimilate new experiences by placing them in the context of a familiar, reliable construction of reality.'[8] By not giving them-selves time to ponder the happenings of the past, and to ask the question 'why?', leavers deprive themselves of a valuable oppor-tunity to put their experiences in perspective.

Employing the familiar analogy of life as a tapestry, Marris describes how an abrupt change of lifestyle causes many of its threads to snap. If, before attempting to join the broken threads and continue the work of weaving, the weaver can stop and view the work to date as a whole, he is much better placed to resume his task with pleasure and confidence. He will certain-ly see that some of the previous workmanship has been shabby, some parts of the design, flawed – yet its very unevenness will, as with an antique carpet, contribute to its unique character and high value. Seen from above, the weaver may clearly discern the dominant elements of pattern and colour in his work. This accomplished, he can then restart, in a good position to introduce other shades of colour and new symbolic forms without destroying the continuity and harmony of the piece as a whole.

* * *

None of this would have made any sense to Jo Grant. She was not so much leaving the military way of life as changing her status within it. Adopting the role of Army wife, she stayed on camp, and it was only when she found herself unexpectedly feeling like a fish out of water, that it began to strike her how great a change she had made.

Jo reckons that she had no time for reflection, going direct from the Army into motherhood. The fact is that there were some months in between, and also some quiet times – even with twins. But she simply didn't *want* to contemplate the end of her Army career.

Jo is still ambivalent about her situation and is acutely aware of a disparity between the image she has of herself and the way in which she is seen by others. Owing to the constant movement of personnel in service life, none of Jo's current friends knew her as a soldier. They treat her entirely as a service wife and as a mum. Half-accepting this, there is nevertheless still a part of her that remains an Army corporal, and it grates when serving personnel explain jargon to her that she already knows, when security issues are alluded to, but not, of course, discussed in her presence, and when apologies are made for 'robust' language. She feels excluded, and yet, she has *had* to change her outward behaviour in order to fit in with other service wives – and her exclusion from the Army 'proper' is a testament to her success in this regard.

Nevertheless, Jo is young, resilient and hopeful. At the time of going to press, she is cheerful, since, out of the blue, she and Chris have heard that they are going back to Germany. Germany has happy memories for them both – where they met, married and worked together. But for Jo, returning not as a soldier but as a wife and mother, things will be very different from the first time around. Is she prepared for this?

Another question: would Jo be more comfortable with herself if she *did* attempt to disengage from her Army persona? An unfair question, since it is her life and she is clearly not disposed to alter the image from which she derives much of her self-esteem. But if she could allow herself to relax her grip on the past just a little, she could perhaps be more open-minded about the opportunities which civilian status could offer her. She is an intelligent, personable young woman and she might just find that a wider world has more going for it than she presently thinks. As it is, her vague discomfort in being *of* the Army but not *in* it seems set to continue for the foreseeable future.

★ ★ ★

It appears, that for many military leavers, the cards, psychologically, are stacked against them. The military does not encourage its members to be introspective (since the needs of the group must take precedence over the needs of individuals). It inculcates the habit of action (since in militarily uncertain situations, inaction, with its attendant risks to morale, is often the most dangerous option of all). With such ingrained behaviours, how can leavers take the first steps towards making a thoughtful transition from one mode of life to another?

They can start doing so by putting themselves in situations where serious self-analysis is permissible – expected even. A sabbatical, a retreat, an expedition, an academic course of study, a journey, a solitary holiday may get the process under way. Anything that will put time and distance – mental and physical – between the subject and the hurly-burly of everyday life. A gap, a chance to be quiet and to let thoughts and feelings settle so that they find their own level and the significance of past events can become clear.

For any of us, at any time, this kind of exercise is useful, but it is doubly so at turning points in our lives. Recalling the achievements to date of which we are most proud, and the happenings that have given us the greatest pleasure may surprise us and will certainly provide much food for thought. For it is likely that many of our peak experiences will bear little relation to conventional notions of success.

Falling in love, the birth of a child, the resolution of a quarrel, a deep aesthetic or religious experience, such things are likely to take their place alongside the achievement of this rank or the holding of that public office. Our perception of satisfaction in life is governed by the underlying value-system to which we relate all our achievements – a value-system derived initially from our family of origin and modified through the medium of our own personality and our life-experience. Bring this into the open and we are well on the way towards defining the kinds of effort, the kinds of aim and the kinds of achievement that make *us* glad to be alive.

Looking steadily at the sorrows and the mistakes of the past fulfils a different function, the function of healing. Facing up to the truth of dissatisfaction; where necessary, apportioning blame and, if it is possible, forgiving the blameworthy (ourselves included) is the only way to lay these things to rest.

Once we are used to paying attention to ourselves, we may not continue to need 'permission' to be reflective, but until that happens, we shall have to go on arranging 'time out' at intervals, to put our thoughts in order.

One other observation: many of the interviewees for this study found the recounting of their experiences to be a useful, even therapeutic, exercise. This is perhaps one area where the military itself could provide tangible help. Already, part of the resettlement assistance offered to leavers is on-going access to employment advice. If, associated with this, it were possible for former servicemen and women to seek a professional 'career review' at a certain time after leaving (say, between two and five years) they could be given just such an opportunity to order their experiences with an informed, interested outsider. This, together with fresh information and career advice, could give new heart to the weary or the depressed ex-serviceman or woman.

Failing this, it is within the capability of any leaver to make a record (written or taped) of his or her own military career – its beginnings, its peaks and troughs and its end. No matter if the exercise seems amateurish or embarrassing, or if the document, on completion, is destroyed; compiling it may be the best way in which a leaver can tell his or her story in its entirety – and telling it is the key to putting its events into a right perspective.

★ ★ ★

Resocialisation

After the move from military to civilian status there follows a learning period. People such as Angus Moorcroft who needed further qualifications to pursue a chosen second career necessarily accepted this. Others, such as Frank Warrell, also accepted a learning period and found it invaluable. And, as he discovered, it was often not new skills that were difficult to acquire but new modes of behaviour.

The habitual projection of confidence, enthusiasm, sociability and busyness so vital in a service environment may seem arrogant and insensitive or boy-scoutishly naive in some civilian settings. The first year or two in civvy street cannot but be an apprenticeship, and it is the wise leaver who acknowledges it and sets out to learn all he or she can. Unfortunately, this period is often marred by resistance to change and a consequent reluctance to learn from civilians whose appearance and manner are unusual by military standards. Frank Warrell maintains that it was not until he stopped judging everyone he met against military norms that he was able to mix easily and to be accepted in civilian circles. Having learned during his 'apprenticeship' to recognise and respect competence in a wide variety of people – including some who would not be tolerated in a military setting – he was ready to demonstrate his own ability in an appropriate, acceptable fashion.

Today, Frank, as an upper-middle manager, is at last permitting himself to feel successful. Since he was interviewed for this study his professional and home life have continued to flourish. At work he has assumed control of a junior management programme – a subsidiary task and not promotion – but the contact it brings with up-and-coming young trainees is giving him tremendous satisfaction.

The chance to make a helpful impact on the lives of others has, furthermore, presented itself in another way. Frank has become a grandfather. Not an intermittent presence, as he was for his own children, (he spent large portions of their young lives at sea) but a round-the-corner, twice-a-week-for-tea sort of grandfather, and he is absolutely delighted. Not that his new status has occasioned any thoughts of retirement. He may be more attuned to quality of life issues nowadays, but he knows that his self-esteem still depends to a large extent upon career achievements and he is not yet ready to rest on his laurels.

Frank is one of those people who gives the lie to the suspicion of some military folk that it is only the 'chattering classes' who value psychological self-awareness. That the introspection this demands is somehow emasculating and abnormal.

Frank is well read and articulate, but comes from a non-aspirational working class family and has had no higher education; he has no unconventional or remotely bohemian tendencies and does not by any stretch of the imagination belong to the 'chattering classes'. He inhabits a down-to-earth world in which he is interested in current affairs, practical economics and in getting things done with a minimum of fuss. Yet this man admits he has always cultivated a greater degree of self-awareness than most. It has patently not made him neurotic or effete. Rather, it has enabled him to be master of his own destiny to quite an extraordinary extent.

★ ★ ★

Changing step is a process, and like any other process, it can get stuck. Although this study points to the disengagement phase as being the commonest sticking point for military leavers, perhaps the most frustrating time to lose momentum is during the re-socialisation period. To have got this far, to know where you want to go but not to be able to get there is desperately dispiriting. Jamie and Beth[9] found this, as did Gavin and Penny[10], Peter and Felicity[11] and also Angus and Jane Moorcroft. Indeed, there may be comfort in the knowledge that many of the most successful adaptors to civilian life interviewed for this survey were at one time in this predicament. Comforting too, to know that the further through the process of changing step you go, the less likely you are to give up.

Resocialisation is not easy, and inevitable mistakes and miscalculations will hamper its progress and may sap the resolve to continue. Jamie and Beth threw in the towel at this point. What might have saved their dreams – and did save the others – was a bold gesture borne of fierce commitment. Gavin's course, Peter's move to the south of England, and Angus's decision to set up his own veterinary practice were hard decisions to take, but raising the stakes, so to speak, enabled them and their families to find the extra concentration and effort they needed to give their plans new impetus.

* * *

Angus has derived great satisfaction from his second career. He has not achieved wealth or power and is far from realising all his aims in the field of animal science, but he is wholeheartedly a civilian, and strong in his attachment to his profession. His children are now grown, his wife Jane is free to pursue her own interests in fine art, and, recently, Angus himself published a research paper in the journal of the British Trust for Ornithology. This has established him as an authority on the ringing and migration of fieldfares and has brought him a step closer to his new goal of full-time research. Though he is now well into middle age, Angus, in sharp contrast to many other respondents, talks emphatically as a man with a future.

* * *

And that is really what this study has been about. Investigating the circumstances, attitudes and ambitions that have given some leavers the incentive to look to the future while others have remained captives of their past.

The results, as we have seen, have been varied and interesting; but if one message has come across loud and clear it is that some leavers are able to, or learn how to, recognise what is truly important to them in life – and having learned it, to pursue it.

Other people, ordinary mortals, tend to take life as it comes.

Fair enough, but few, if any, leavers can simply shrug off the institutionalising effects of their years of service. They have been, expensively, painstakingly conditioned *by* the military, *for* the military, and deconditioning doesn't just 'come' as a matter of course.

Disengagement from membership of the armed services and resocialisation into a new role is a long and at times uncomfortable process, but another message of this study is that the end result is worth striving for. Adaptation requires thoughtfulness and vision, steadiness of purpose – and time. It does not require an IQ of lofty proportions, only the will to think long and hard about the kinds of things (different for each person) that have made, do make, and will make life eminently worth living. It demands that the leaver should attempt to determine for him or herself the types of activity that, in the past, have brought contentment, and the sorts of endeavour that have sparked off long-term enthusiasm and effort. The quest for new employment and for satisfying activities outside work can then proceed – slowly but surely – seeking compatibility with these determining ideals.

Because, whatever individual leavers are inclined to think that living is primarily *for* – the accumulation of wealth, the search for pleasure, mental challenge, personal growth, wisdom, the love or esteem of others, any or all of these – there is no doubt that most would *like* to experience a full and a rich life according to their own perceptions of such, with a firm sense of purpose, right up to the end.

This cannot be achieved by clinging to the past, but the letting go is frightening, and the building of a future is hard work. Undaunted, however, the prize of that future, 'the gift of continued life', is supremely worth the winning.

APPENDIX

Basis for Structured Interview

The format which follows, appears as it was drawn up and as it was analysed, that is, roughly in chronological order. However, only the first four interviews were conducted in this order, as subjects tended to be reluctant to move on from the recollection of their military experience to the recounting of subsequent events. Therefore, the interviews gradually settled into a pattern which began with a discussion of the present (A), moved into the Resocialisation phase (E) and then went back in time to Confrontation (C) and Disengagement (D). Military experience was discussed towards the end of the interview (B), which concluded with two 'gut reaction' questions (F). Interviews were recorded in note form and transcribed at the earliest opportunity.

A. *The Present*
a. Occupation. Describe. (Allied to military? Professional? Self-employed? Employed – transferable skills? Employed – retrained? Unemployed?)
b. Age.
c. Marital status.
d. Children.

B. *Military Experience*

a. In which arm of the forces did you serve?
b. Between which dates?
c. What was your rank on leaving?
d. What was your branch/trade/specialism?
e. What did you do before you joined the military? (School? Work? Higher Education?)
f. What originally attracted you to military service? (Military family?)
g. Training. To which aspects of military life did you adapt easily; which were more difficult?
h. Operations. What are your most vivid memories of military service?
i. Family. What were the major pros and cons of the military years for them? (Did they 'follow the flag'?)
j. Was there any aspect of yourself that you felt was not catered for in a military life?

C. *Confrontation*

a. Can you pinpoint a time when you first seriously contemplated the prospect of leaving or having to leave?
b. Did you leave prematurely or on completion of a term of engagement? (Degree of suddenness?)
c. Did you go or were you pushed? (Degree of willingness?)

D. *Disengagement*

a. During your last tour of duty did you have any kind of break from routine to allow you to think through your situation?
b. What was the attitude of your family at this time?
c. Rites of passage. Was there a *formal* marking of your departure from the Service?
    Any event which privately marked leaving for you? How did you feel?
    Were your family involved?
    What marked the departure for them?
d. Immediately afterwards. (Deliberate bridging moves. *False starts.*)
e. Low points? Regrets?

E. *Resocialisation*

a. How much was there to learn? (Studentship? Training? Probationary/Learning period? New qualifications? Languages?)

b. Feedback. Nature of the workplace – describe typical daily interaction with others.
   Have you felt it appropriate to dress differently/behave differently?

c. Role models. How clear? Have you consciously sought them?

d. How much has your lifestyle changed?
   Materially – possessions – house, car, furniture etc.
   Leisure activities – time out, holidays, etc.
   Circle of friends. Values?

e. How much contact do you still have with things military?

F. *Quick Questions*

a. Just suppose a favourable offer were made to you to rejoin – what would be your reaction?

b. How contented/satisfied are you with your life now?

Further Reading

D.A. Abbott & G.H. Brody 'The relation of child age, gender and number of children to the marital adjustment of wives', *Journal of Marriage and the Family 47*, 1985.

F.M. Andrews & S.B. Withey, *Social Indicators of Well-Being*, Plenum, 1976.

M.J. Apter, *The Experience of Motivation*, Academic Press, 1982.

Michael Argyle, *The Psychology of Happiness*, Methuen, 1987.

Karen Armstrong, *Through the Narrow Gate*, Macmillan, 1981.

Karen Armstrong, *Beginning the World*, Macmillan, 1983.

P.L. Berger, *The Homeless Mind*, Penguin Books, 1974.

John Bowlby, *Attachment and Loss*, Vols. I, II, & III. Hogarth Press, 1969, 1973 & 1980.

James Campbell, *Gate Fever*, Weidenfeld & Nicolson, 1986.

R. Chester & J. Peel, *Equalities and Inequalities in Family Life*, Academic Press, 1977.

S. Cohen & L. Taylor, *Psychological Survival*, Penguin Books, 1972.

Erving Goffman, *Asylums*, Anchor, 1961.

Erving Goffman, *The Presentation of Self in Everyday Life*, Penguin Books, 1971.

Pat Howes, *Becoming a Parson: Change of life-plan and the voice of God*, published as a chapter in Frank Musgrove *Margins of the Mind*, Methuen, 1977.

Further Reading

Michael Ignatiev, *The Russian Album*, Chatto & Windus, 1987.

Thomas Jenkins, *We Came to Australia*, Constable, 1969.

Ruth Jolly, *Military Man, Family Man: Crown Property?*, Revised edition, Brassey's, 1992.

Brian Keenan, *An Evil Cradling*, Hutchinson, 1992.

Anthony Kenny, *A Path from Rome*, Sidgwick & Jackson, 1985.

John Lawrence & Robert Lawrence M.C., *When the Fighting is Over*, Bloomsbury, 1988.

T.E. Lawrence, *Seven Pillars of Wisdom*, Jonathan Cape, 1935.

Erich Lindemann, 'Symptomatology and management of acute grief', *American Journal of Psychiatry*, vol 101, 1944.

R. Lynn (Ed), *Dimensions of Personality*, Pergamon, 1981.

John McCarthy & Jill Morrell, *Some Other Rainbow*, Bantam Press, 1993.

Peter Marris & Anthony Somerset, *African Businessmen*, Routledge & Kegan Paul, 1971.

Peter Marris, *Loss and Change* (Revised edition), Routledge, 1986.

Peter Marsh & Desmond Morris, *Tribes*, Pyramid, 1988.

Roger Middleton, 'Artists: Precarious Identities in Private Worlds', published as a chapter in Frank Musgrove *Margins of the Mind*, Methuen, 1977.

Jan Morris, *Conundrum*, Penguin Books, 1987.

Colin Murray Parkes, 'Bereavement and mental illness', *British Journal of Medical Psychology*, vol 38, 1965.

Frank Musgrove, *Margins of the Mind*, Methuen, 1977.

Frank Parkinson, *Post Traumatic Stress*, Sheldon, 1993.

Mark Spilsbury, Institute of Manpower Studies, 'Transferability of Skills and the British Armed Forces', Paper to the ESRC Research Seminar Series, *A Farewell to Arms?*, 17 January 1994.

V.W. Turner, *The Ritual Process*, Penguin Books, 1974.

J. Veroff, E. Douvan & R.A. Kulka, *The Inner American*, Basic Books, 1981.

Terry Waite, *Taken on Trust*, Hodder & Stoughton, 1993.

Michael Yardley & Dennis Sewell, *A New Model Army*, W.H. Allen, 1989.

Chapter Notes

Chapter 1

1. Peter Marsh and Desmond Morris, *Tribes*, Pyramid, 1988.
2. Frank Musgrove (ed.), *Margins of the Mind*, Methuen, 1977.
3. Pat Howes 'Becoming a parson: change of life-plan and the voice of God', in Musgrove, *Margins of the Mind*.
4. Karen Armstrong, *Through the Narrow Gate*, Macmillan, 1981; *Beginning the World*, Macmillan, 1983; Anthony Kenny, *A Path from Rome*, Sidgwick & Jackson, 1985.
5. Pat Howes 'The Homosexual as stranger', in Musgrove, *Margins of the Mind*; Jan Morris, *Conundrum*, Penguin Books, 1987.
6. Roger Middleton, 'Artists: precarious identities in private worlds', in Musgrove, *Margins of the Mind*.
7. Thomas Jenkins, *We Came to Australia*, Constable, 1969; Michael Ignatiev, *The Russian Album*, Chatto & Windus, 1987.
8. Peter Marris and Anthony Somerset, *African Businessmen*, Routledge, 1971.
9. S. Cohen and L. Taylor, *Psychological Survival*, Penguin Books, 1972; James Campbell, *Gate Fever*, Weidenfeld & Nicolson, 1986.

10. Brian Keenan, *An Evil Cradling*, Hutchinson, 1992; John McCarthy and Jill Morrell, *Some Other Rainbow*, Bantam Press, 1993; Terry Waite, *Taken on Trust*, Hodder & Stoughton, 1993.
11. Frank Musgrove, 'A Home for the disabled; a change of tense', in Musgrove, *Margins of the Mind*; Erving Goffman, *Asylums*, Anchor, 1961.
12. John Bowlby, *Attachment and Loss*, Hogarth Press, 1969, 1973 and 1980; Erich Lindemann, 'Symptomatology and management of acute grief', *American Journal of Psychiatry*, vol. 101, 1944; Colin Murray Parkes, 'Bereavement and mental illness', *British Journal of Medical Psychology*, vol. 38, 1965.
13. Peter Marris, *Loss and Change*, Routledge, revised edn, 1986.
14. Ibid.
15. See note 6.
16. Michael Argyle, *The Psychology of Happiness*, Methuen, 1987; F.M. Andrews & S.B. Withey, *Social Indicators of Well-Being*, Plenum, 1976; R. Lynn (ed.), *Dimensions of Personality*, Pergamon, 1981; M.J. Apter, *The Experience of Motivation*, Academic Press, 1982.

Chapter 2

1. *Matthew* 10:14.
2. There were, of course, people for whom wanting to fly or to go to sea was a reason, but not the main reason, for joining up. They are not included here.
3. Any study of this kind is likely to encounter a good many 'success stories' – probably a disproportionate number. Successful people tend to keep in touch with former friends and colleagues, making them easy to trace. They also tend to be more than willing to submit to questionnaires and interviews.
4. This group were unusual in being able to articulate a range of aims, hopes and ambitions. Most people are far less clear about the things they want from life.
5. This predates predominantly graduate entry.

Chapter 3

1. Bernard Dodd.
2. Erving Goffman, *Asylums*.
3. Karen Armstrong, *Beginning the World*.
4. Anthony Kenny, *A Path from Rome*.
5. A little under half the respondents (26–28 out of 62) found it hard to stop talking about their military experiences once they had begun. Of these, 12 individuals were definitely unenthusiastic about their lives since leaving. This is almost a fifth of the total, which, though the study is small and cannot claim to be strictly representative, is a worryingly high figure.
6. S. Cohen and L. Taylor, *Psychological Survival*.
7. James Campbell, *Gate Fever*.
8. Frank Musgrove, 'A Home for the disabled: a change of tense'.
9. John Lawrence and Robert Lawrence, MC, *When the Fighting is Over*, Bloomsbury, 1988.
10. Sgt Arthur Wilde RM quoted by Dudley Pope in *Battle of the River Plate*, Secker & Warburg, 1987.
11. Sqn.-Ldr. J.J. Pook, from *Freestyle Mudmoving in the Falklands* (unpublished)
12. See note 9.
13. Lt. Col. I.R. Gardiner, RM, from a lecture to the Tri-Services Staff Colleges, 1989 (unpublished).

Chapter 4

1. Twenty respondents described in some detail how their being deprived of an expected position had triggered their departure from the military.
2. All three services have schemes for promoting selected men and women from the ranks, mid-career, into the junior eschelons of the officer corps of their service. In the Navy, successful candidates serve on the Special Duties List, in the RAF, they become Branch Officers, and in the Army they may advance either through gaining a Quartermaster's Commission or through the Late Entry

scheme. In all circumstances candidates will have served for long enough in the ranks to have distinguished themselves professionally, but the inevitable result of this is that they are, in most cases, significantly older as junior officers than their direct-entry counterparts. Few are able to progress beyond the rank of lieutenant-commander, major or squadron leader.
3. Peter Marris, *Loss and Change*.

Chapter 5

1. Ruth Jolly, *Military Man, Family Man: Crown Property?*, Brassey's, 1992. See Chapter 3.
2. Gill Z. Cowden, *Postbag* (Army Wives' Journal), Autumn, 1994.
3. Joyce Grenfell, *Opera Interval*, EMI Records, 1978.
4. John Lawrence and Robert Lawrence, *When the Fighting is Over*.
5. There were no reported adverse reactions from the families – immediate or extended – of service*women* preparing to leave. This may be owing to the small number of servicewomen interviewed, but it may also reflect the innately conservative attitude of the military community towards women, which, despite rapid movement in the rules governing equality, is changing only slowly. It is difficult for career women in the forces to be taken seriously as such, however readily their professional abilities are acknowledged. Their leaving to pursue a civilian career or to produce children is accepted without question in a male-dominated environment. Dr Alison M. remembers: 'I could have stayed . . . but . . . my mind was made up. Nobody tried to change it, least of all my family.'
'It's a *man's* life in the Army' seems to reflect the view of the majority when it comes to long-term careers. Whether a daughter's or sister's service in the forces fails to forge a link with her family or whether there is from the start an expectation that the link will be temporary is impossible to say. There certainly appears not to be the same level of

family identification with the Service to which a female is attached as there is to that of a male.

Chapter 6

1. Why is this? When asked, most people replied that they couldn't be spared from busy jobs, but talking to administrators who *run* resettlement courses it would seem that many leavers wait until the last minute before thinking about courses, and are perfectly willing to take no for an answer when they finally get around to applying. So why? Perhaps it feels disloyal to be preparing too thoroughly to quit. Perhaps it is denial, not facing the frightening prospect of finding employment in civvy street. Perhaps it is misplaced pride, a suspicion that accepting help is tantamount to admitting that one cannot organise one's own affairs.

2. HIVE: an acronym standing for Help, Information and Volunteer Exchange. Military HIVEs play a generally equivalent role to the Citizens' Advice Bureaux found in British towns and cities.

3. Peter Marris, *Loss and Change*; (see particularly Chapter VI: 'The Conservatism in Innovation'.

Chapter 7

1. Traditional occupations were those where subjects were (*a*) employed, or self-employed in a *very* similar capacity to that in which the subject worked in the military, or (*b*) in public service, employed by central or local government, or (*c*) working for a security firm, or (*d*) working for a charitable foundation, or (*e*) as the employee of a professional or similar limited-membership group. Non-traditional occupations were those where subjects were (*a*) self-employed (in reality, not notionally while in practice working on a long-term basis for a single employer) in a capacity other than that for which military training was given, and/or (*b*) acquired competence via a significant period of formal retraining. For intermediate occupations, see note 3.

2. Mark Spilsbury (Institute of Manpower Studies), 'Tranferability of Skills and the British Armed Forces', paper to the ESRC Research Seminar Series, *A Farewell to Arms?*, 17 Jan. 1994.

3. In this instance there were two main difficulties. First, the intentionally wide variety of subjects' new occupations did result in a statistical over-representation of unusual career paths. Secondly, it was impossible to assign some jobs clearly to the traditional or the non-traditional category, necessitating the creation of an 'intermediate' category. The resulting figures were that from 63 interviewees, 19 were employed in clearly non-traditional work and 25 in clearly traditional work, six were not employed, leaving 13 in intermediate occupations. These included, for example, a number of teachers and a number of self-employed people who were, as civilians, making their living in a new capacity but from knowledge and skills learned in the military.

4. Pat Howes, 'The homosexual as stranger'. Ten subjects were interviewed, eight men and two women. Their age range was 23–38 and their occupations were: an artist, a railway porter, a social worker, two students, a clerk, a window-dresser, a researcher, an industrial executive, and a teacher of handicapped children.

5. Pat Howes, 'Becoming a parson: change of life-plan and the voice of God'. Twelve subjects were interviewed, their average age on ordination was 39. There were two former architects, five engineers, a clerk, a textile chemist, a businessman, a plumber and a policeman. All were married with children.

6. Roger Middleton, 'Artists: precarious identities in private worlds'. At least 10 subjects were interviewed, a majority being aged between their late twenties and late thirties. Previous occupations included a bus driver, a teacher, a textile designer, an industrial designer and a clerk. Of the 10 named subjects, only two could definitely be said to have achieved a career change which was both materially successful and emotionally satisfying.

Chapter 8

1. Michael Argyle, *The Psychology of Happiness*.
2. Ibid. Chapters 3 and 4 are of particular relevance here.
3. D.A. Abbott and G.H. Brody, 'The relation of child age, gender and number of children to the marital adjustment of wives', *Journal of Marriage and the Family*, Vol. 47 1975; J. Veroff, E. Douvan and R. A. Kulka, *The Inner American*, Basic Books, 1981; C. Walker, 'Some varieties in marital satisfaction', in R. Chester and J. Peel (Eds.), *Equalities and Inequalities in Family Life*, Academic Press, 1977.
4. Michael Argyle, *The Psychology of Happiness*.
5. Ibid.

Chapter 10

1. T.E. Lawrence *Seven Pillars of Wisdom*, Jonathan Cape, 1935.
2. Case history: Nick P., see Chapter 4.
3. Case history: Sandra J., see Chapters 4 and 7.
4. Case history: Malcom W., see Chapters 4 and 8.
5. Case history: John T., see Chapters 2 and 5.
6. Case history: Peter, see Chapters 6 and 9.
7. Case history: Geoff, see Chapter 7.
8. Peter Marris, *Loss and Change*.
9. Case history: Jamie and Beth, see Chapter 9.
10. Case history: Gavin and Penny, see Chapter 7.
11. Case history: Peter and Felicity, see Chapter 6.